DON'T
QUIT
YOUR
DAY JOB

One Bad Dude, with Ted Jefferson (1978, Master's Press,
paperback, 1979, Baker Books)

The Lynchings in Duluth (1979, Brasch & Brasch, titled
They Was Just Niggers), reissued in 2000 under present
title by Borealis Books, an imprint of the Minnesota
Historical Society Press

The Man From Lake Wobegon (1987, paperback 1986, St.
Martin's Press)

One Shining Season (1991, Pharos Books)

Chronicles of Aunt Hilma and other East Hillside Swedes
(1991, North Star Press)

The Pocket Guide to Minnesota Place Names (2002,
Minnesota Historical Society Press)

Indians in the Arborvitae (novel, 2002, Green Bean Press)

*A Sawdust Heart, My Vaudeville Life in
Medicine and Tent Shows,* with Henry Wood
(2011, University of Minnesota Press)

Zenith City: Stories From Duluth
(2014, University of Minnesota Press)

*Don't Quit Your Day Job: The Adventures of a Midlist
Author* (2018, Holy Cow! Press)

DON'T QUIT YOUR DAY JOB

THE ADVENTURES OF A MIDLIST AUTHOR
A MEMOIR

MICHAEL FEDO

Holy Cow! Press
Duluth, Minnesota
2018

Author photograph by Judith Fedo.

Book and cover design by Anton Khodakovsky.

Printed and bound in the United States of America.

First printing, Fall, 2018

ISBN 978-09986010-6-9

10 9 8 7 6 5 4 3 2 1

The publisher is grateful to Felicia Schneiderhan for her careful editiorial attention to the contents of this book.

Holy Cow! Press projects are funded in part by grant awards from the Ben and Jeanne Overman Charitable Trust, the Elmer L. and Eleanor J. Andersen Foundation, the Cy and Paula DeCosse Fund of The Minneapolis Foundation, the Lenfestey Family Foundation, and by gifts from generous individual donors. We are grateful to Springboard for the Arts for their support as our fiscal sponsor.

Holy Cow! Press books are distributed to the trade by Consortium Book Sales & Distribution, c/o Ingram Publisher Services, Inc., 210 American Drive, Jackson, TN 38301.

For inquiries, please write to: HOLY COW! PRESS, Post Office Box 3170, Mount Royal Station, Duluth, MN 55803. Visit *www.holycowpress.org*

WITH LOVE TO MY FAMILY:

Wife, *Judith*

Daughters, *Kimberly and Kacey*

Grandsons, *Cameron and Wyatt*

Granddaughters, *Madeline, Chelsea, and Cally*

Great-grandson, *Maximus*

Great-granddaughter, *Teagan*

CONTENTS

PREFACE

A STANDARD DEFINITION FROM WIKIPEDIA AND OTHER SITES TELL us that midlist books refer to volumes appearing in the middle of a publisher's list. They do not become bestsellers, and publishers don't expect them to attain that success. Midlist books rarely receive much promotion or advertising support.

Publishers and book trade people used to assume that such books would typically sell between 10,000 and 25,000 copies. While most authors today would be delighted with those numbers, most books published in America rarely approach 10,000 "units" (as books are referenced these days by sales representatives), yet they are not labeled "bottom list." Doing so might disrespect said authors. Thus, these also are designated midlist. After all, even publishers don't want to be considered as presenters of bottom-list books. For our purposes, we'll call authors of published books that don't approach bestseller stratosphere, "midlist authors," and I am in that company.

Let it also be known, however, that so-called midlist books, and backlist books—tomes that have been published perhaps years earlier, but continue to sell modestly—occupy about eighty percent of book store shelf space. Without midlist titles, there would be no bookstores.

Might an author aspire to be merely a midlist writer? In certain instances, probably yes. Authors writing local or regional histories, technical and scientific books, or biographies of minor political figures, for examples, have no expectation of huge sales, and understand from the start, their books are likely targeted for specialized readerships and libraries. Some might never be placed in bookstores. However, these books add to the body of knowledge, and are worth publishing, but no one—authors or publishers—believe they will be big money-makers. Most often, such works are produced by nonprofit presses run by historical societies and universities, where large monetary returns on sales of books are not anticipated.

The contents of this book reflect a real-world look at my own decades-long career as a published freelance writer of articles, essays, short stories, a novel, poetry, and eight nonfiction books. In other words, widely published, but not a household name. Thus, I'm typical of regularly published writers who are off the grid when it comes to name recognition with the reading population. Midlist in every respect, but that doesn't mean there haven't been engaging encounters and experiences along the way.

The general reader may be interested in the journey of an author who works as hard as those more recognized writers without receiving fame (and fortune). This same journey may be instructive and useful to those readers/ writers who aspire to publication.

Let the sojourn begin.

CHAPTER 1

AUTHORITIES AND EXPERTS MAY BE WRONG

MANY YEARS AGO, AS A COLLEGE SOPHOMORE, I ENROLLED IN A short story writing course at the University of Minnesota-Duluth, taught by Harry Davis. It was the only creative writing class I ever took and I got a C in it. According to Dr. Davis, my stories lacked verisimilitude and were weak in character development. Heedless of my instructor, over the subsequent decades I've published ten books—including one novel—and scores of articles, essays, short stories, and a few poems, each one a refutation of Prof. Davis's discouraging words. I may have become a writer to dispel his perception that I wasn't one.

Every week Dr. Davis would read aloud and discuss short stories from his creative writing students. One day he selected mine—the story of a young man in war. Sighing occasionally during the rendering, Harry looked up at the end and said, "Class—what's wrong with this story?"

"Pulp fiction, man," said a slouching-in-his-seat kid in the back. "Sounds like somebody trying to write for money." Heads nodded.

"Perhaps," Professor Davis said. "Has this author ever been to war? Class—it's a cardinal rule that writers write what they know and this writer didn't do that. This story lacks verisimilitude."

Following Dr. Davis's appraisal, others jumped in with seconding opinions. Most reconfirmed its dearth of verisimilitude (a new word for me that day) and stated that my blatant attempt at commercialism negated it as literature.

Strangely, I wasn't devastated. I somehow—perhaps arrogantly—intuited that Harry and his acolytes were wrong.

It was true that I had no experience with war or prisons or disintegrating families—subjects addressed in other stories I submitted. But what I understood, even before I took myself seriously as a writer, was that writers are not necessarily limited to writing only what they know; they write to discover what they don't know, to discover and articulate what they think about topics and issues. In short, writers are risk takers and evolving learners, not restricted to narrow parameters of life, as personally encountered. And way back then, I somehow knew these truths, and that made me less vulnerable to the scoldings by the teacher and fellow students.

Over the years, the specter of that professor hovered as I composed. With each publication I felt an urge to send the story, essay, or book off to him. But I resisted. Several years after I'd graduated, I learned from a fraternity brother currently enrolled in Harry's class, that another of his former students had recently published an essay in the now long-defunct *Reporter* magazine. This was a noteworthy achievement, as it was one of the country's premier intellectual journals, rivaling the *Saturday Review, Harper's,* and the *Atlantic Monthly.* Harry, who hadn't been impressed with that student author some years earlier, was also dismissive of his essay. "What it shows," he said, "is that even a mediocre writer can publish if he hangs around long enough."

Actually, there's some truth in Dr. Davis's last statement. Persistence indeed pays off. Richard Hooker's *Mash* was rejected twenty-one times; *The Dubliners* brought James Joyce twenty-two turndowns; Jack London received 600 rejections before making a sale; Gertrude Stein submitted poems for twenty years before earning an acceptance; and crime novelist John Creasey was nixed 754 times prior to publishing 564 books.

Scores of editors and professors have wrongly assessed fledgling authors. E. C. Mabie, a 1930s University of Iowa theater professor, savaged a student's play in front of his playwriting class. The piece was written by Tennessee Williams, and Prof. Mabie later refused to write a recommendation for him when Williams applied for a graduate fellowship.

Many readers recall the sad tale of John Kennedy Toole, whose *Confederacy of Dunces* posthumously won the Pulitzer Prize in 1981, twelve years after the author's suicide. Toole had struggled for years to interest publishers, before his determined mother, with Walker Percy's influence, persuaded the Louisiana State University Press to issue the novel in 1980. Would any of the multitudes of editors who passed on the manuscript admit to being wrong after it won the Pulitzer?

That's hard to say, but I don't think any of my published writings would have validated me in Harry Davis's eyes either. He might have said that I was just lucky or persistent, maybe both.

On the other hand, Harry taught me, albeit inadvertently, that each rejection of my work was not necessarily a reflection of its worth—or mine; rather it indicated that an editor was wrong, and I always maintained that somewhere down the line another editor would get it right.

The above essay was written for the discontinued journal, *A View from the Loft*. The thoughts expressed in the piece were the result of more than forty years of reflecting on this author's writing life and experiences. But let's go back to the where it all began.

In mid-May 1956, I was attending the annual Minnesota High School Press convention at the Curtis Hotel in Minneapolis with Myrtle Rogina, adviser to the Duluth Central High School *Spectator*, and several other juniors who would be *Spectator* editors the next year. I recall little of the convention itself until Friday evening during the banquet, when I found myself seated next to an attractive female student journalist from Osseo High School, with whom I'd become deeply engrossed in non-journalistic conversation.

Suddenly, Central colleagues were urging me to get up on stage; I'd won an award, they said. I didn't believe them. Assuming they knew I hadn't been paying attention to the program and wanted to embarrass me, I didn't move. It wasn't until Mrs. Rogina rose halfway from her chair and directed me to stop fooling around. "They're waiting for you," she said, rolling her eyes. "Stand up and get your prize."

I had placed first in the sports writing competition for high school journalists with a story I didn't even remember writing. It was a report on the previous winter's Central victory over rival Denfeld High School in basketball. I had no idea that the story I'd written as a favor to Bill Jacott, the *Spectator's* sports editor who could not attend the game, was out of the ordinary. Bill had submitted the piece to the competition without mentioning it.

My award was a commemorative pen and certificate—both long-since lost. What wasn't lost, however, was the notion that perhaps I could write.

I'd always done decently in classes that required expository writing and drifted through school with only minimal effort. But this was different; students who were serious about writing were in this competition, and I had managed first place. "Professional quality writing," said one of the judges—a professor from the University of Minnesota's journalism department—extending his hand.

I had even wondered why Bill Jacott recommended me to succeed him as sports editor the next year since I'd written only a handful of other pieces for the *Spectator* my junior year. I took the post knowing a long list of extra-curricular activities might be necessary to counterbalance my middling grade point average and assure college admittance. I was already playing football and baseball, had been a class and club officer, participated in forensics and theater, so adding "editor" seemed prudent, especially since I possessed a first-place sports story award for Minnesota high school journalists.

When I returned to my table following acceptance of the honor, the young lady from Osseo had vanished. Win a few, lose a few. . . .

I examined the citation, which stated my article was a clear and well-written account of a basketball game, embracing the highest standards of Minnesota high school journalism.

The award enforced the notion that I wrote better than most of my peers, but so what? That I would over time evolve into a writer of stories, essays, articles, poems, and books was never even a second thought, let alone first.

During my senior year at Central, I busied myself with athletics—football and baseball—while concomitantly editing the *Spectator* sports page, and contributing a column titled "Sports Shorts." In addition, each page editor was to alternately prepare a monthly report from the school to the Friday Teen Page published in our local evening daily, *The Duluth Herald*. Sports never figured in these pages, and I found myself bored by having to develop 200-word articles about projects undertaken by the Boys and Girls clubs or new sewing machines purchased for the clothing classes.

Despite a personal lack of interest in some assigned topics for the Teen Page, my stories were noticed by Orville (Bud) Lamoe, the *Herald-Tribune's* executive editor, who thought I had promise. He offered to help me get admitted to the prestigious Medill School of Journalism at Northwestern University in Evanston, Illinois. Not having given much thought to becoming a journalist, I didn't appreciate the extent of his generosity. When I broached the offer to my father, Dad was dismissive. "Do you know what a reporter makes at the *Herald* and *Tribune* here in town?" I didn't. "$35 a week," Dad said. "You want to get a college degree and earn a lousy $35 a week?"

I didn't, and so declined Mr. Lamoe's assist to enroll at Medill. At the time I and those around me held limited visions for my future and the futures of my brothers, David and Stephen. Our parents, products of the Great Depression, valued stability and security above everything. A college degree was worth much more than what cub reporters of that era earned, and it would be a colossal waste of time to pursue a newspaper career.

It never occurred to them or to me that Lamoe might have had a clue about where J-school training could take me. Maybe *Life Magazine*, or the august *New York Times*, perhaps anchoring radio or television newscasts. No. Dad assumed I'd always live in Duluth, and with a journalism degree might one day earn up to $85 dollars a week with the hometown paper.

Instead I took a $250 scholarship—which in those days paid for tuition, fees, and books for an entire year, and declaring no major, enrolled at the University of Minnesota-Duluth.

At the same time, however, I landed a part-time job across the St. Louis River in Superior, Wisconsin reporting on high school football at the daily *Evening Telegram* for seven dollars a game. Though it was the first time I was paid for writing, the engagement with journalism didn't last. I declined an offer to remain at the *Telegram* to cover winter sports; it would have meant giving up dating on Friday and Saturday nights.

That summer, after accumulating mediocre grades as a freshman, and with my scholarship not renewed, I enlisted in the Air National Guard. I was enrolled in a school for personnel specialists at Lackland Air Force Base in San Antonio, Texas. Students attended classes from 6 AM until noon Monday through Friday. But instead of time for resting and goofing off after lunch, we were assigned to work details that might involve picking up cigarette butts on the parade grounds, emptying sacks of dirty laundry, or the dreaded KP, where we'd scour pots and pans until after the evening meal. We might also be sent to paint warehouses. I found none of this appealing, so one afternoon, during a break, I located the office of the base newspaper and offered my services, telling them of my high school award and sports reporting experience with the *Evening Telegram*.

Without asking to look at writing samples, the editor hired me, but since a sports editor was already in place, I was given general assignments, including covering weekend entertainment on the base. (Regular airmen, as opposed to those of us still in training, nearly always had weekends off. Those in the advanced training status might manage every other weekend.) But this was still better than grunt work, and I happily accepted.

I recall my first-ever celebrity interview. On the heels of her hit recording of "The Wayward Wind," Gogi Grant gave a concert on the base. Off-stage, we chatted for more than thirty minutes as I developed a profile for the paper. Several weeks later, the vocal group, Four Preps, of "Twenty-Six Miles," and "Big Man" fame, joined the California Air National Guard and were sent to Lackland for basic training. I met the somewhat harried lads in the newspaper office about a week after their arrival. They'd just received "the haircut" and with locks shorn, seemed quite out of place. But showmen that they were, they kicked it in for the interview, which was a large feature in that week's paper.

Five months later when my schooling ended and I was set to return to Duluth, the editor of the paper, a master sergeant, who was pursuing a Ph.D. in history during his off-duty hours, shook my hand and said, "You're a decent writer. You should try to change your job from personnel specialist to journalist."

CHAPTER 2

FINDING THE FUNNY

AFTER THE AIR GUARD STINT, I RETURNED TO COLLEGE AND floundered through another year, but found my interest piqued by literature. However, I pursued a speech major with only an English minor—fortuitous, as it would turn out, because my friends who harbored writing ambitions and majored in English found themselves teaching junior or senior high school classes—an endeavor that left little time for pursuing their own ambitions. Few of them ever attempted to publish, though several placed poems in obscure literary journals.

The speech major, by the way, was a haphazard choice. I'd been informed by my adviser during my sophomore year that I would not be allowed to enroll the next quarter unless I declared a major. Speech emerged only because I'd already taken three classes and earned a B in each of them, with what I deemed minimal effort. I was, it seems, averse to rigorous toil, and speech might enable me to further avoid it.

I did some creative writing as a student announcer on KUMD-AM, the newly formed closed-circuit campus radio station. It was then a low-wattage, student-staffed AM operation that today has a professional crew. I teamed with David Tester to do half-time "color" commentary at college basketball games. I put "color" in quotation marks, because our commentary had little to do with color or commentary, for that matter. During each halftime, we interviewed two notable UMD season ticket holders: Winston Churchill and character actor Walter Brennan. David managed an excellent impersonation of Churchill, while my Walter Brennan was at least passable. As Churchill, David would talk about whichever team was trailing at halftime, and would always conclude with a riff on the famous "Finest Hour" speech.

Should the team come from behind and win the game, David's inevitable conclusion was "If (name of college here) lasts a thousand years, they will surely say 'This was her finest hour.'"

And my Walter Brennan was always befuddled, clearly not comprehending what basketball was all about, wondering why the bouncing ball was called a dribble, when dribbling, as far as he was concerned, was something babies did. "Players runnin' 'round helter-skelter," I'd say, "could learn a thing or two from even them lousy, smelly sheepherders, by cracky." Taking after Jonathan Winters's *Maude Frickert*, I on occasion was Granny, who lusted after the strong, handsome young players on the floor, not caring a whit about the score. She admired the sturdy legs of the young boys, and their physiques, why she'd never seen the like. You get the picture. The sketches were mostly off-the-cuff, but were loosely outlined as the game's first half unfolded. Fun stuff, but well, sophomoric, which might have been somewhat complimentary for a couple of freshmen. I was honing a comedic sensibility though, that I would later develop in short stories and in sketches performed by my folk-singing partner Dan Kossoff and me during our brief sojourn working coffee houses, clubs, and campuses in the early 1960s.

Mostly we did parodies of current hit songs, and silly, sometimes satirical stuff, without having an intellectual grasp of defining what we were doing. Years later I came across an observation in a 1939 book my wife, Judith, found when our local library was getting rid of old, rarely circulated volumes.

This one, by Milton Wright, was titled *What's Funny—and Why*, where Wright observed, "Humor is a state of affairs that is enjoyably incongruous."

Looking back at the erstwhile folk music gig, and beyond, into the writer I've become, the statement certainly worked for me, since incongruity so often leaps out to those of us who attempt writing humor.

But I couldn't articulate it then. It took a few decades for my writerly brain to identify what works for me when I try to write funny—well, amusing, anyway. After publication of a batch of stories following my early retirement from college teaching, I was able to analyze why humor was a métier for me. Here are some examples:

Item: Shortly after beginning guitar lessons my wife, Judy, idly remarked that she'd like to learn to play the blues.

Item: Two men are conversing in a working-class tavern. One tells the other that his son is taking a pottery class in college, then adds, "He's a funny kid. Never liked sports."

Item: A brief *Los Angeles Times* report stated that stunt performers in films were miffed at not receiving Oscar recognition from The Academy of Motion Picture Arts and Sciences.

Item: At a tony sushi restaurant, where I'm entertaining a friend who lives in a sparsely populated, remote region of the state, he tells me there's just one tiny tavern back home serving nothing but frozen pizza and jerky.

Each of these episodes provided the bases for humorous short stories that editors purchased. What turned these routine snippets into stories of any kind, let alone amusing ones? Incongruity.

Pulitzer Prize-winning author Robert Olen Butler used headlines from supermarket tabloids as inspiration for his short story collection, *Tabloid Dreams*. In one of them, "Husband Returns in Form of Parrot," the narrator, a cuckolded man, has died. He is reincarnated as a parrot, and is purchased by his widow. He thrashes in his cage, scattering seeds during his wife's affair with "a guy. . . whose Adam's apple is as big as my seed ball." In Butler's skilled hands, readers have no difficulty suspending disbelief at the improbability of this story.

"For something to be funny," Milton Wright asserts, "it must bear a resemblance to something that is wholly sensible. This resemblance may be utterly artificial, but it must be there." It's there in Butler's story, and readers can accept an implausible premise as "sensible."

Since reading Wright's tome, I am conscious that the story's thesis must make sense within its parameters. To discover incongruities that work I ask,

"What if . . .?" and let my imagination fill in the blank.

For example, the thought of the straight-laced middle-aged mother of my daughters singing and playing the blues was incongruous. But not quite as skewed as the final draft of a story I titled, "The Ladies of West Rarington Falls Get Down," involving a group of elderly white suburban dowagers who want to study the blues and try to relate them to their life experiences.

The incongruity of women in their sixth and seventh decades determined to sing and play the blues tickled me more than having my fifty-year-old wife resolved to master the form.

In this story, published in the *North American Review*, the ladies engage an aging Delta blues singer to conduct a workshop for them. However, the ladies don't really relate to his songs about hunger, loneliness, and infidelity. They prefer applying the blues to more personal topics: what to do about six competitive granddaughters, each of whom expects Grandma to purchase Girl Scout cookies from her alone. Or how dead-heading petunias contributes to winning blue ribbons at county fairs.

Then from the overheard barroom conversation I extracted this incongruity: What if patrons of a working-class bar discussed art and literature with the same intensity they brought to their profane harangues about pro football or five-card stud?

The result was "Art's Place," printed in *America West Airlines Magazine*, where a group of regulars sip Calvados and Grand Marnier instead of beer and whiskey, while passionately discoursing on the arts.

The story opens with a creamery employee baiting the proprietor by telling him that Marcel Duchamp could paint rings around Mark Rothko, a particular favorite of the bartender. "That Rothko couldn't hold Duchamp's palette," he says. "He couldn't even stretch Duchamp's canvas."

Other characters enter the fray, and a fight is about to erupt after one customer calls another a closet Walter Keane freak. At the story's end there is good-spirited bonhomie, with Art, the bartender, setting up drinks on the house.

"To peaceful, passionate discourse," he announces, raising his Cinzano cocktail. "To Rimbaud, Rauschenberg, and Man Ray."

"Hear, hear," chorus the patrons, glasses raised, arms around each other's shoulders, Ezra Pound's inscrutable *Cantos* playing on the jukebox.

In humorous fiction, there must be just enough incongruity, just enough deviation from things as they ought to be—but not too much. In "Art's Place," it's believable that if men were to talk about modern art and literature instead of sports, they'd sound like the customers at Art's place.

A news item about stunt workers not receiving Oscar recognition resulted in my asking, what if there were Academy Awards for minor, behind-the-scenes supernumeraries in the film industry?

"Lunch with Jackie Cliff, Oscar Winner" (published in the *North American Review* and reprinted in *America West Airlines Magazine*) was my response. This story, framed as a newspaper interview with the first best boy (the assistant to the gaffer or head electrician) to receive an Academy Award. Jackie Cliff describes his climb to the pinnacle of best boydom over a Spago's restaurant lunch of angel-hair pasta with porcini and chevre. Between bites, Cliff reveals how he'd forgone a promising high school football career to run lights for his senior class play, and was smitten by show business.

Cliff pays homage to his mentor, an elderly gaffer, and brags that he received his Oscar at a much younger age than Steven Spielberg. In the end Cliff asserts he's entitled to more consideration from the film industry. He says, "I'm gonna call my union rep first thing when I split this joint and tell him, hey, that's it. I'm entitled to something better. From now on, I'm a gaffer or I'm gone, baby."

The sushi episode occurred several years ago. A friend's comment about the small, main street saloon back home started me thinking incongruously. What if that tavern were replaced by an upscale sushi bar? How would local gentry react sampling alien comestibles that "tasted like the inside of a fishbowl," instead of their favorite pepperoni pizza?

The result was "Gunnar Sundstrom's Sushi Bar," which also appeared in the *North American Review*. Here, morose, rural rustics grouse about having to endure sushi and oshinko pickles. The owner confesses that he too misses the defunct Buckhorn Bar, but insists that customers will adjust to the new place. "Hey," he says, "change keeps you on your toes. Besides, you can't stop progress."

Another story was inspired by Paul McCartney's attaining knighthood at age fifty-four. Do musicians ever get too old to rock and roll? Beyond this, what kind of music would senior citizens of tomorrow want to hear? I wrote "At the Stairway to Heaven Elder Care Center," about a former accordion-saxophone duo who stopped playing treacly chestnuts for seniors in favor of sixties and seventies rock and roll, which the old folks loved, but was upsetting to attendants who now had to deal with boisterous antiquarians hitting on each other in the corridors, and shouting "Hell no, we won't go," when it was time for bed. "Stairway" was included in the initial reincarnation of *December* literary quarterly.

Some beginning writers are less concerned with plot and character development than with such details as how many sentences should be in a paragraph. I've never thought of writers or artists as being dominantly left-brained, but what if there were an association of left-brained writers?

In my story "At the Left-Brained Literary Convention" (published in *Lynx Eye*), the author of *Fiction by the Numbers* tells his left-brained audience that writing is merely putting one word after another. He says that stories and essays should always be seven pages long—the Biblically perfect numbers—and that writer's block can be overcome simply by typing "The" at the top of the screen. "After that, almost any noun will do, and voila, you're off to the races."

Naturally, not every "What if?" question results in a salable story. I've written some clunkers too. But writers of humorous fiction are risk-takers. They need not be afraid to stretch credulity for the humor genre.

Editors who may have definite opinions on what they like in mainstream fiction waffle a good deal over funny fiction. They're often less confident about humor because they suspect that what makes them laugh may not even elicit a faint smile from someone else. Also—and this is only my opinion, unsubstantiated by quantitative analyses—I suspect that many first readers may be intimidated by bosses who appear serious (cranky?) and don't pass along humor, fearing the boss will not laugh, thus putting their fledgling careers at risk.

In fact, I was once told never to label a submission "humorous," but instead let editors decide if it's funny. The fact that so many editors passed on John Kennedy Toole's hilarious Pulitzer Prize-winning *Confederacy of Dunces,* further attests to their attitude toward humorous fiction.

Many of my stories have not been amusing to editors; in fact, "Art's Place" received eighteen form rejections spanning two years before appearing in print. The rejection of a story may simply be the fact that an editor doesn't see incongruities as you see them. If you feel an affinity for humor, don't give up. With humorous fiction, as with other writing, persistence, developing a voice for dialectics, and a modicum of talent often pays off.

CHAPTER 3

BREAKING INTO PRINT

THINKING BACK ON IT NOW, I MAY HAVE DEVELOPED THE URGE TO put drollery on paper during the summer of 1961, following my junior year in college. At the time, my father was president of the Duluth Teacher's Association, and the union's attorney was Gerald Heaney, a Democratic Party operative in Minnesota, who later became a federal judge.

I'd been unsuccessful in landing a local summer job that year and Dad said something to Heaney, who mentioned it to his good friend, Sen. Hubert Humphrey, who used his influence to get me a labor position in Glacier National Park. It was fascinating to be in the mountains midst the company of bears both black and grizzly, along with elk, mountain goats, deer, coyotes, wolves and others. I caught cutthroat trout in my free time, and in exchange for a restaurant meal, wrote letters back home for other park employees. The several missives I composed for friends were attempts to inhibit the interest of hometown females in my pals. The guys weren't interested in serious relationships with those women, but didn't want to bluntly say so.

It started with Bob, a high school counselor from Kansas, who was pursued more aggressively than he wished, by a home economics teacher at his school. "I'd like to discourage her without being rude or hurting her feelings," he said. "I don't know how to do that."

I said I could perhaps dis-enthrall the lady, and asked to see a recent letter from her. He produced one in which the woman wrote, among other things, that she missed him despite his cornball sense of humor, and had been hanging out with another single gal from the school. She said that he hadn't said much in his letters about what he was doing in the park and how the job was going. She signed off with "As ever, Sharon."

"Is she inferring something with 'as ever?'" I said.

"Yeah, I think so," Bob said. "She's a nice gal, but . . . ."

I responded with a two-pager for Bob, playing off her comment about corny humor. In the letter, Bob said he was spending his free time trying to get marmots and skunks to eat out of his hand, and in dealing mostly unsuccessfully with the latter, spent a great deal of time in the shower and had been evicted from the bunkhouse. He was currently sleeping in the back of a pickup truck. He also hadn't been feeling well of late, and just yesterday working at Lake McDonald, he'd thrown up all over his foreman's hard hat after breakfast.

Bob didn't sign off with "as ever," but scrawled, "Happy Trails."

She didn't respond, and Bob was pleased. I got a prime rib dinner reward at the East Glacier Hotel.

My letter in his behalf so impressed Bob that he suggested I do the same for a couple other fellows in the employees' bunkhouse.

I rather enjoyed crafting these silly letters, and would later learn that Alex Haley also took pleasure in similar endeavors. Before publishing the mega-selling memoir, *Roots*, he'd been a Coast Guard journalist. Prior to that, though, as a Coast Guard kitchen orderly, he wrote love letters for his mates to their ladies back home. The success he enjoyed from these spurred him to look to a writing career after he retired from the military. I wonder if it was those letters from Glacier Park that nudged me a bit. Hey, I maybe can do this. I can write a mirthful missive when I put my mind to it.

Despite graduating with a speech major, I was hired by the Superintendent of Schools in Duluth, to teach tenth-grade English at Denfeld High School. I stayed for two enjoyable years, during which time I also served as tennis coach and assistant football coach. I left the position because I thought I was too young to be ensconced in pleasant stability.

I toyed with joining the Peace Corps, but Fred Meitzer, a theater professor at UMD, suggested I go to graduate school first. However, gaining admittance proved challenging. Several universities, noting my marginal undergraduate transcript, and borderline scores on the Millers Analogy test and Graduate Records Exam—requisites for admission into most grad schools—declined my application. Fred used his influence with his alma mater, the School of Speech at Kent State University, to help me secure an assistantship with the department for the 1964-65 academic year.

Earlier, as a UMD sophomore I became enamored with the burgeoning popularity of folk music and learned a few chords on the guitar and participated in campus hootenannies organized by Jerry Music (later Lorenzo Music, creator of the Bob Newhart television shows, Emmy-winning writer of the Smothers Brothers Show, and most notably, the voice of Garfield the cat in the cartoon series).

I eventually teamed up with Dan Kossoff, and we spent vacations and weekends playing clubs and campuses throughout the Midwest, as a sort of Smothers Brothers knock-off.

This experience initiated my inadvertent sojourn as a freelance writer. During our two-year run, we survived on chutzpah more than talent. I speak for myself here not Dan, who was a much more skilled performer than I, and who carried me because I could craft parodies and comic sketches.

Our hoped-for career as entertainers stalled, however, when we learned that without a hit record or even a recording contract, we'd gone about as far as we could, and almost simultaneously we both decided to attend grad school. Dan went to Kansas, and I was headed for Ohio.

However, I often regaled friends and acquaintances with anecdotes about that brief show business sojourn, and some encouraged me to write them down. One well-meaning chum said "Write it all up and send it to *Reader's Digest*. I heard they pay a thousand bucks for funny stories."

My assistantship at Kent State would net me about $40 per week. That thousand dollars loomed very large indeed.

Six weeks before I left Duluth for Kent, I wove my folk music anecdotes into four and a half typed pages and sent them off to *Reader's Digest*. Ten days later my manuscript was returned with a note that said my submission didn't meet their present needs.

If not now, I thought, perhaps a few weeks later. I mentioned the note to another friend, who informed me that I'd received a form rejection slip: a polite way of telling me the manuscript not only didn't meet present needs, but future as well. Nada. Forget it.

Then he told me that writers expect rejections, and they simply send their manuscripts elsewhere and hope for better luck. So off it went again, and again, and again, and back it came with similar form rejection slips.

I'd been settled in my gloomy one-room basement apartment on Powdermill Road in Kent for several months when I opened my mail to find another rejection slip, but also a handwritten note from an editor of a men's magazine. "You don't write badly," was his opening, before he continued, saying in a long paragraph that my submission was off the mark for his magazine, but he had little doubt it would find a home elsewhere. "Consider a careful rewrite," he wrote, "and send it out again. Good luck." My next submission, following his advice, produced my initial sale to a now long-defunct magazine. The acceptance note concluded with "Enclosed, find our check for $60." Oh, frabjous day, calloo callay!

After cashing the check and treating myself to a sirloin steak at a small neighborhood diner, I began to contemplate what publication (and payment) might mean. Here I am netting $40 a week for twenty hours of supervising undergraduate announcers at the student-run campus radio station, whereas I earned $60 for a three-hour stretch of thinking about then typing up four-and-a-half pages and selling those pages to a magazine.

Despite my class load and assistantship responsibilities, I certainly had more than three free hours each week to develop four- or five-page essays. Surely, I could sell at least one of them a month and live rather grandly on the $60 plus my wages.

I dutifully began crafting short, and what I thought to be humorous pieces that were submitted and submitted and submitted ad infinitum.

The now nearly forgotten humor writer, Richard Armour, gave a speech at the university. He had published more than sixty books over his career—poems, columns, essays—most notably *It All Started With Columbus* and *Twisted Tales From Shakespeare*. At Kent he seemed quite the amiable gentleman, and since I'd been attempting my own satirical essays, I sent him one for critiquing the week after his campus lecture. I didn't realize that this might have been an imposition, and when I mentioned it to my adviser, he said, "Don't expect a reply. Dr. Armour is a very busy man, you know."

About a month later I received my manuscript back from Armour, with detailed comments both about what he liked and what was wrong with the story (quite a bit, actually). I shelved it, and nothing else sold during my grad school days, but there was a literary experience of sorts. As assistant to the faculty supervisor of the campus station, WKSU, I was responsible for some of the programming. One afternoon, a freshman named Harold came to my office. He said he had a recording from his godfather that I might find interesting. When I asked what it was about, Harold said his godfather was an older, retired gentleman telling stories about his life. I should listen to it, Harold said, and put it on the air.

I was less than enthusiastic, partly because Harold didn't elaborate, and I didn't probe. I assumed the stories were whimsical yarns told by an old codger about his years on the farm, and probably not of any interest to those outside the family. But Harold insisted I take the tape, which I deposited in the bottom drawer of my desk.

Several weeks later Harold strolled in and asked what I thought of his godfather's stories. "Geez, Harold, I just haven't gotten around to it yet."

A couple weeks later he made another inquiry. To put an end to the badgering I said I'd listen to it that night. It turned out Harold was named after his godfather, Harold Latham, editor-in-chief of MacMillan Publishing Company, and the tape contained a chapter in his yet to be published memoir, *My Life in Publishing*. The recording detailed Latham's trip through the South looking for new talent, and his encountering Margaret Mitchell, who reluctantly surrendered a massive manuscript to him. He read it on the train heading back to New York. The reading was about how he discovered *Gone With the Wind.* Our tiny campus station in northern Ohio had the scoop on that story, when I scheduled it for broadcast two nights later. When I asked Harold why he didn't tell me Latham was his godfather, Harold said, "I thought you'd appreciate the surprise."

I didn't make another sale for fifteen months by which time Kent State University had granted my M. A. in broadcasting and theater, and I was teaching lower division radio and introductory speech classes at Marietta College in southeastern Ohio. This time the check for a short story totaled $50.

What happened during those fifteen months of composing what were deservedly unpublishable pieces, was that I acquired the writer's discipline of spending time nearly every day at the typewriter, attempting to write short stories and essays. Additionally, I consulted publications like *Writer's Digest* and *The Writer,* both for advice on the craft, as well as potential markets for the sort of writing I was doing.

Beyond assisting the director of the campus radio station at Marietta, I hosted a weekly discussion/interview program, while teaching nine hours per week. Among the guests I interviewed for the program were actor John Carradine, authors Harry Golden and Harry Caudill, whose book *Night Comes to the Cumberlands* allegedly provided the impetus for President John F. Kennedy's War on Poverty program. I also hosted the revered poet Richard Wilbur.

Golden was promoting his book *A Little Girl is Dead,* about the lynching of Leo Frank, a Jew falsely accused of assaulting a young white girl. I had not yet finished that book, but had read his best sellers *Only in America* and *For Two Cents Plain.* When I brought up *For Two Cents Plain,* he put down his cigar and mentioned his friend Carl Sandburg once said to him, "'Harry, a book is very precious. There's nothing like holding your own book in your hands for the very first time.' And Carl was right."

I've often thought of that whenever a new edition of mine is delivered and unwrapped, and I heft it for the first time. It is always a glorious, tactile pleasure.

Caudill's massive book arrived only the day before he was scheduled for the program so I had no opportunity to do more than read the cover copy and skim a few chapters before meeting him. He entered the studio and we shook hands. He was a rangy man with large hands as I recall, and a thick Kentucky dialect, which would cause me brief consternation during our interview.

His book was an indictment of industrial practices in Appalachia, and during the interview he continued his criticism of the profiteers who pillaged the region through strip mining and other endeavors that devastated the land. He was able to carry the interview with a few leading questions from me. Then he said something that threw me, relating how difficult life was for people in "Squaylor."

In my cursory read I had not come across Squaylor. There was Boone and Whiteville, and other communities impacted, but Caudill mentioned Squaylor several times. I was about to ask the location of Squaylor, but Caudill bore on, emphasizing a point, which was fortuitous. When he paused, and I was about to finally get him to tell me where Squaylor was, I stopped short. The Squaylor he was discussing was not a noun, not a place, but a condition: squalor. I've often envisioned what might have ensued if I'd asked him where Squaylor was, and his look of befuddlement and a likely response; "Why it's everywhere." And my return confusion about how a physical location could be everywhere. I can still feel the flush when the pale lifted on that sunny winter afternoon.

I remember discussing writing and the writer's life with Richard Wilbur. Following his graduation from college, he went to New York where he envisioned pseudonymously writing pot-boilers—crime and romance novels—to support himself while crafting his "important and meaningful" poems. He failed at those efforts, he said, because he couldn't manage popular genres. "All writing is hard work," he said. "You can't write down to an audience; your work will seek its own level. It required as much time to write bad crime and romance stories as it did to develop my serious poems. I finally came to realize that instead of wasting my time by trying to write what I found uninteresting, I needed to write what I knew was important to me."

And a good thing too, for Wilbur went on to win countless honors for his poetry, his translations of Moliere's plays, and for contributing lyrics to the Leonard Bernstein musical *Candide*.

There was another author who visited my radio program—a Vietnamese exile whose name I've forgotten—to discuss his new book supporting America's involvement in the tragic conflict. At the time my own thoughts on the war were ambivalent; I didn't think that America's position was way out of line, and I suppose I timidly assented to the author's strong defense of his thesis. I know I never challenged him on the air.

However, intervening months saw my view evolve into opposition to U. S. intervention, though I was not an activist. But even uncertainty didn't cut it with the college administration. Marietta's president was an Annapolis graduate who'd had a distinguished naval career before earning a Ph.D. and entering academia.

At some point nearing the end of the first semester, a campus organization was soliciting signatures from students and faculty in support of American troop intervention in Vietnam. I did not sign the petition, but explained to the young men who approached me that I hadn't yet made up my mind.

As it turned out, this was a mistake. In fact I may have been the only faculty member not signing on, and in that small, insular environment with a number of faculty members teaching at their alma mater, I felt like a pariah for not signing. I know the president was not pleased. Short story; I was terminated, and as a non-tenured instructor, I was not entitled to appeal. My department head simply said, "This isn't quite working out," then promised to write a recommendation for me as I sought other employment.

He did, but his was a strongly negative assessment, and it kept me from landing two jobs after being interviewed by department heads at other institutions. Both said I was a very strong candidate, but all consideration vanished after my references were forwarded, which included the Marietta evaluation.

(Suspecting subterfuge, under the guise of seeking work in public television in Jacksonville, Florida, I had my records sent to a friend there, who forwarded them to me. After requesting removal of the negative review, I quickly obtained a position at Stout State University—now University of Wisconsin-Stout—in Menomonie.)

My arrival in Menomonie coincided with sale number three. A year had passed since achieving my second publication. This sale went to *Ellery Queen's Mystery Magazine.*

The story, "My Brother's Keeper," won the magazine's "First" award and payment of three-cents per word for the 2,500-word piece. An assistant editor there said she looked forward to seeing more of my stories. I thought perhaps this was my niche, so I began churning out mystery and crime stories and sending them in turn to the Ellery Queen magazine and to the old *Alfred Hitchcock's Mystery Magazine*, neither of which gave a shred of encouragement to the six or seven stories I submitted.

I finally sold another to the British magazine *London Mystery* and received twelve pounds for it (roughly $30 at the time).

I probably tried another half-dozen of those without success, so I gave up on crime stories, deciding the two I did place were likely aberrations. Truth be told, I was not an avid reader of crime fiction in the first place.

I tried writing pulp western stories then, but abandoned those as well after two or three attempts. I never read westerns, so whatever possessed me to assume I could write them? I should have learned from Richard Wilbur's advice.

Instead, I dusted off the piece Richard Armour so graciously critiqued, rewrote it according to his suggestions, gave it a new title, and voila! It sold the next time out.

Hearkening to what this very successful author did for me back in 1965, I have also seldom refused to read work handed me by tyro writers. I offer a caveat though: I might not like the story and would they be offended if I didn't? You'd think hopeful authors would be grateful even for negative (helpful?) reactions, but I've had several young writers decide they could live without my assessment after all. For the record, to my knowledge, none of those former aspiring authors have experienced publication.

CHAPTER 4

THE STORY
BEHIND A STORY

EANWHILE ONE AFTERNOON IN THE CABIN JUDITH AND I were renting on Tainter Lake in Colfax, Wisconsin, back in 1968, I wrote a science fiction story titled "The Carnival." The story was something of a gift, practically writing itself, and I completed the 2,000-word draft in a single afternoon.

It was about a future society that dealt with overpopulation by staging carnivals where participants faced possible death on the midway rides. A bit of tweaking the next day, and off it went in the mail.

Scholastic Magazines purchased the story, and it appeared in publications used as classroom supplements by junior and senior high school English teachers.

For all rights to the story I received a princely sum of $200. Despite being warned in various writers' magazines not to sell all rights to a story, the Scholastic fee was much higher than I'd ever received for a work of fiction before, and was also more than I earned in a week at my day job teaching at Stout. Besides, how many reprint offers does a writer get anyway? It was a no-brainer and I happily cashed the check.

Following publication, I received letters from students who loved the story. A fifteen-year-old girl from Upper Darby, Pennsylvania wrote: "This is the best story I've ever read. . . . You must be brilliant. Did you write any others like it?"

At the time, I hadn't, and try as I might, I could never capture the magic of "The Carnival" with the four or five science fiction pieces I later attempted. So much for brilliance.

Fast forward to 2006. I Googled myself—a periodic exercise I've undertaken ever since learning that a couple of my stories had seen foreign publication thirty years earlier without my knowledge and no payment. If Google posts activity regarding my name, I'm ready to contact publishers who used my material on the sly. I have collected two checks I wouldn't have received without the online listings.

Then about three years ago I found my name on an Isaac Asimov web site. Someone had asked about a story he'd read many years before in high school. He couldn't remember the title of the story or the author, but it was about a boy who went to a carnival where people might be killed on the rides. Someone had replied that "The Carnival" was the story's title, written by Michael Fedo. Further, the story could be found in a textbook anthology titled *How to Read A Short Story,* published in 1980. I wasn't aware of that text; perhaps Scholastic Press had attempted to locate me and send copies of the book, but I'd moved five times in three states since the 1968 sale of the story.

In the anthology, my story appears between literary giants Nathaniel Hawthorne and Edgar Allen Poe. More stories in the anthology were written by Mark Twain, Anton Chekov, O. Henry, Guy de Maupassant, Kurt Vonnegut, and others. I was the only unknown selected for inclusion, probably because the story generated such interest among middle and high school students and their teachers. The story is considered nearly a genre classic, occasionally referenced as influencing sci-fi novelists during their formative years. It has been taught in American classrooms for nearly fifty years as I write this book. In fact, an editor who published a previous book of mine said she remembered the story from her freshman year in high school more than thirty years earlier.

I posted a note on the Asimov web site indicating surprise that my story resonated after all these years. English teachers responded saying they still taught "The Carnival," and asked if pupils could email me with their reactions and questions about the story.

I spent an afternoon or two each week during the last semester of that academic year responding to kids' queries. Some of them were writing papers about my story. A few of them sent me copies of their work, and nearly all suggested meanings I'd not considered myself when writing the story. I had no idea I was making sage comments on the human condition; I simply thought I was writing what I hoped would be an entertaining story. One energetic and creative crew of high school boys actually turned my story into a rather avant-garde short film, accessible on-line.

I continue to receive emails from students and teachers about "The Carnival." Recently I was surprised to see the story had a Wikipedia entry that reads in its entirety:

"The Carnival" is an American short story written by Michael Fedo. The story concerns a nation that constructs a deadly amusement park to remedy its over population problems. It focuses on a young boy (Jerry) who wins a ticket to the titular Carnival. After he arrives, he realizes the park's true nature while on a ride called the "Thunder Clapper" that electrocutes some of its passengers. The story ends as the protagonist is being thrown off a ride called the "Whirl-Away" to his death.

I've also learned that "The Carnival" had long ago been published in Italy, Germany, and Brazil. I saw none of these magazines, which alas, had ceased publication. None of them paid for republishing.

But I'm not complaining; I relinquished additional considerations when I signed the agreement with Scholastic. Needless to say, had I foreseen "The Carnival's" future, I would have negotiated for First North American Serial Rights only.

On the other hand, how many mid-list writers get to see one of their short stories in print fifty years following initial publication and continue to receive fan mail for it?

Incidentally, "The Carnival" was resurrected in April 2013 in a new digital anthology, *Playing With Fire,* by Third Flatiron Press. It still comes up on online chat sites, with people mentioning this carnival story they read years earlier in high school. Some draw comparisons between it and Shirley Jackson's classic *The Lottery.*

CHAPTER 5

A LOOK AT CHARACTERS

I SPENT THE ACADEMIC YEARS 1966-69 AT STOUT, AND AFTER CLASSES and department meetings, wrote short stories. I sold only one more after "The Carnival," a humorous fiction called "A Light Lunch Will Be Served," also to *Scholastic Magazines*, while placing several others in small literary quarterlies, none of which paid cash but gave contributors copies of the magazines.

I also wrote and published two one-act plays. My arrival at Stout had coincided with the director of theater, Noel Falkofske, planning a sabbatical for the next year, and since I was already on board, I was asked to temporarily assume his position. His wife, Karin, a theater director of high professional standards, wanted to direct original work in the college's experimental workshop theater, and she invited me to contribute. Though I'd acted in plays, and had even directed in graduate school, I'd never considered writing for the stage.

Karin was encouraging, so I submitted a draft, which she analyzed and suggested rewrites of sections, and these suggestions continued into rehearsals for the play, which took a quote from a Hemingway short story as its title: "If a Four-Letter Man Marries a Five-Letter Woman (Of How Many Letters Will Their Children Be)?"

When the piece came off rather well, Karin requested another, and I managed a comic, experimental work called "The Tie That Binds." Again she helped shape the piece, and it too received a warm reception. It also got the attention of a theatrical agent in New York, who liked my work, but wanted me to write a full-length play. "We can shop the one-acts after you've had some productions with a full-length play," she said.

That should have been encouragement enough, but as with detective and science fiction, I apparently didn't have a two-act play in me. At least not then. My efforts seemed futile, and after several starts stalled and were not completed, I abandoned future attempts to write plays.

Discouraged at my inability to please the agent, and unable to successfully market short stories except to non-paying literary magazines, some of which were run off on those old ditto machines, I needed to find a means to reinvigorate my writing.

Then I noticed a section in the Sunday *St. Paul Pioneer Press* newspaper that was produced for Wisconsin readers. It featured stories of interest to residents of western Wisconsin communities bordering Minnesota.

One of my students had captured a number of national water skiing championships, unusual at the time because he competed against athletes from Florida and California who had access to water all year long, while this young man was limited to three or four summer months. I interviewed him and sold the profile to the *Pioneer Press* for $40.

Thus began a two-year relationship with the newspaper as a regular contributor to the Wisconsin pages. Depending on word-length, I received anywhere from $35 to $50 per submission, usually managing one or two of those per month.

During this period, I hadn't entirely stopped producing short stories, but I didn't write many, preferring to concentrate on supplementing the family income for the three of us. Daughter Kimberly arrived during my third and final year at Stout. I kept my fiction brain active, however, by joining a few other faculty members who also aspired to publication.

One friend, Scott Chisholm, who had placed several dozen short stories and poems in literary quarterlies, was miffed that none of his efforts landed in the "slicks"—those mainstream magazines like *The New Yorker, Esquire, McCall's,* or *Redbook.*

He was determined to hit one of the slicks so he began spending a couple hours each afternoon in the college library where he analyzed the types of sto-ries published in these major magazines. He finally concentrated on *Redbook* because it ran two stories in each issue, and he determined to resolve their for-mula. Scott studied every story that appeared in that magazine over the past year, finally announcing, "I think I've got it," over coffee in the campus lounge.

Several weeks later he finished a short story and sent it off. Within six weeks the story was returned, but the editor had commented on the submis-sion. In a handwritten note at the bottom of the rejection slip she'd scribbled: "We regret we are declining this one, but it sounds too much like a *Redbook* story."

Scott later taught in Utah, and wrote a wonderful book about his experi-ences walking the trail the early Mormons traversed before reaching Salt Lake City. He published *Following the Wrong God Home: Footloose in the American Dream* in 2003, four years before he died.

There was another author who came to Stout the same year I did. I met him one morning during the first week of class, when he plopped himself down at the table in the student center where I was having coffee with a mem-ber of the English department. After my tablemate introduced me to Peter Kavanagh, this wooly-haired, florid-faced Irishman insisted surely I would be familiar with him.

"Me name is Peter Kavanagh," he persisted, repeating it rapidly in a thick brogue.

"I'm sorry," I said. "Should I know you?"

"Well, there's no need for farther discussion now, is there?" he huffed. "And you a so-called di-rector of theater." With a dismissive wave of his hand, he turned away, sullenly spooning sugar into his tea.

Later I learned that Dr. Peter Kavanagh had been hired to teach fresh-man composition at Stout. His initial irritation with me stemmed from my not being acquainted with his books—most notably *The Irish Theater* and *The History of the Abbey Theater* (where the plays of W. B. Yeats, John Synge, and Sean O'Casey were staged), which O'Casey lavishly praised in a front-page review in the Sunday *New York Times Book Review*.

Further, Peter's brother was the renowned Irish poet, Patrick Kavanagh, whose work was equally foreign to me. Peter no doubt expected any thespian worth his greasepaint to be cognizant of important scholarship on the Abbey, and because I wasn't, during the next several months he derisively addressed me as "that doctor of dramatics."

After learning of his tomes, I approached Peter to inquire about the Abbey's iconographic dignitaries. "That's in the past," he said abruptly. "It's done, and farthermore (sic), it no longer interests me."

Then one night he attended an evening of Samuel Beckett one-act plays I directed but left during intermission. "The heat is tremendous in here," he carped. "More people might be inclined to attend your plays if the custodians moderated the furnaces." That he perennially wore the wool turtleneck sweaters of Irish fishermen beneath tweed jackets seemed to him not a contributing factor to our overheated auditorium. He was off then, down the corridor dragging his preschool daughter, Caitlin, behind him in a wagon. She was his constant companion in classes and at other events.

The next day he stopped by my office and asked if I was familiar with *Life* magazine. "They wrote me up," he said. "On the matter of John Quinn, about whom I assume you know nothing. You could look it up if you've a mind to," he added, hurrying off to meet his students in the adjacent classroom.

I didn't take his barbs seriously because he baited many campus bigwigs too. He confronted the head of the English department at a public meeting. "Why in God's name," he roared, pointing an accusing finger, "is there such a thing as a required remedial English course for master's degree students? Haven't they larned the bloody tongue by now? What sort of institution is this? What in God's name have I come to? And aren't we all of us ashamed?"

The department chair patiently explained to Peter that Stout's primary mission was to train young men as teachers of industrial arts and young women as home economists for Wisconsin public schools. The administration held that student who might perform well in the auto mechanics lab, or who could oversee banquet halls with panache, should not be thwarted in their career pursuits because they lacked grammatical acumen. If they wished admission to graduate programs, however, it was imperative that their writing skills be honed to passible mediocrity.

"This is not to be believed," Peter moaned as he slumped in his seat.

His pupils received fairly rigorous assignments, and he sent batches of their themes to Stout's dean, a man named Agnew, to prove that students were capable of turning out serviceable prose when it was expected of them. The dean never responded, arousing Peter's considerable contempt. "That man will regret ignoring me," Peter asserted. "I am not a tolerant man when ignored."

It was impossible to ignore him at committee meetings, as he was quick to proclaim dozens of points of "arder," prolonging tedious sessions and greatly vexing committee members.

Once he protested at a humanities division gathering that it seemed endless and accomplished nothing. "Why don't we all agree to forget about meeting in future?" he suggested. "Give everyone a bloody rest from all the bickering."

An assistant professor rose to the occasion. Deftly mimicking Peter's brogue, he said, "Well now, if you'll be after quietin' your own tongue for five minutes, Dr. Kavanagh, we might have adjourned thirty minutes ago."

Chastened, Peter grinned and sat down. There were no more points of "arder."

Peter's tempestuous nature intimidated both Stout faculty and students. The latter often wouldn't express opinions in his presence. "I won't have ye sayin' you're afraid to speak up," I once heard him bellow from his classroom next to my office.

His bluster had to have piqued our dean. Whenever Peter spied Dr. Agnew entering the student union cafeteria, he would stand and loudly announce, "Here comes that harse's ass, Ag-NOO." Cringing, other faculty at Peter's table could only hope that Ag-NOO hadn't noticed them.

At one budget planning session, Peter was present with Caitlin squirming in his lap. Scorning the picture books and fruit slices he'd brought to pacify her, she began tugging his ears and twirling his hair. For a while he softly hummed Gaelic tunes to distract her. Then he abruptly stood and, placing the three-year-old in the chair next to him, barked, "Be still, will ye now. Can't you see I'm tryin' to kick up a row?"

Meanwhile I located a copy of *Life* dated February 8, 1961. The piece on Peter was titled, "A Wild Irishman's Literary Wars" and dealt with his losing battle with the New York Public Library over the ownership of papers and letters from the estate of John Quinn.

The library sought an injunction against Peter, then a scholar and printer residing in New York, to keep him from distributing a hand-set and bound collection of Quinn's letters. The library maintained that Peter had violated a signed agreement not to publish material from this collection.

Quinn had been a prosperous New York lawyer who conducted prolific correspondence with then emerging writers and artists and frequently gave them money to assure the continuance of their work. Among Quinn's beneficiaries were Yeats, James Joyce, T. S. Eliot, and Georges Rouault.

By the time of his death in 1924, Quinn had amassed hundreds of letters and notes from important writers and artists; he bequeathed them to the New York Public Library. Courts construed his will as banning publication in any form until 1988.

"To me the pledge not to publish had no validity at all," Peter told the reporter from *Life*. He argued that Quinn's letters belonged to anyone with a passion for art and literature. They contained revelations that biographers would need to complete their manuscripts.

The Quinn papers were only available to accredited scholars who signed a compact stipulating that they refrain from publishing anything from the collection. Moreover, scholars were not permitted to possess writing material when viewing the documents.

Life reported that Peter spent thirteen days examining the letters, memorizing salient passages. Then, leaving the room, he would write them down. Back in his loft, he set type for the book that would take him into court against the library's army of attorneys.

Peter had fashioned his printing press from scavenged materials including a sewing machine and auto jack. He considered himself primarily a printer who happened to have a Ph.D. in literature and taught in universities.

He produced 119 copies of the book, which he intended to distribute to other scholars and libraries.

In court, Peter made an impassioned plea for understanding and appreciating his cause, concluding with, "This world is divided between decency and hooliganism, and by its action, the New York Public Library has clearly sided with the hooligans."

He failed to convince the judge, whom he addressed as "Your Lordship," and was ordered to bring all but two of the books, which he could keep for himself, to court the next day.

That evening Peter hacked copies of the book to bits with a shoemaker's knife. The following morning he emptied burlap sacks containing chunks of the opus on the judge's desk.

He seemed pleased that I had read the magazine's feature and allowed the trace of a smile. "So you see, I am a rather famous, or shall we say infamous, man," he said proudly. Then leaning in, he added that he'd withheld a third book and spirited it to a Dublin library.

Meanwhile there were rumblings around campus that the dean was considering sacking Peter. The chair of the education department reported that administrators thought Peter didn't fit in with Stout's rural constituency. His raging, disparaging notions would be better suited to New York, where he'd last lived.

In two years he'd managed to antagonize every administrator and a number of faculty colleagues, berating them for not having read great literature and for failing to involve themselves in serious scholarship. "But of course, that's no surprise," he said. "For ye don't even read the scholarship your betters are producing."

In the end his presence at Stout would not be tolerated, and despite his academic and professional credentials, the long-circulating rumor came to pass. Peter was terminated at the end of the 1968 academic year.

He was truly shocked by his dismissal and said it was beyond comprehension.

"But Peter," someone said. "Think about it. You can't call the dean who hires you a horse's ass and not expect him to react. Especially since you don't have tenure."

"But he is a harse's ass," Peter protested. "We know it and he knows it. I am a man who never lies. He shouldn't be so damned sensitive."

That was the last I'd see of Peter Kavanagh, though years later I heard he had returned to Ireland, where he edited Patrick's final poems and published a biography of him.

He died in Ireland in 2006 three months shy of his ninetieth birthday. Before learning his death, from time to time I'd wondered whether, after leaving Wisconsin, Peter might have found a measure of satisfaction from his work outside of academia, either writing or printing. I don't think he'd have wished that for himself, though. His milieu was agitation; he was a man for whom turbulence was a *raison d'etre*. A more likely scenario would have found Peter in the middle of a row he'd kicked up himself in a Dublin pub, perspiring, gesticulating, and thumping a cane against the floor, a hyperactive young grandchild pulling his lips, inserting fingers in his ears.

CHAPTER 6

HITTING *THE NEW YORK TIMES!*

I RESIGNED FROM STOUT AT THE END OF THE 1969 ACADEMIC YEAR and accepted a job with the department of instructional resources at the State University College of New York in Plattsburgh. While this position paid better than the one I was leaving, I failed to calculate the freelance income earned from my articles for the St. Paul paper, and the education-oriented articles I'd been placing in *The Christian Science Monitor*. Living costs were higher in far upstate New York, and by moving, I'd lost those semi-regular markets. Financially the move became a lateral one instead of a step up.

I was hired at Plattsburgh to fill a vacancy that the department was about to lose if the position wasn't filled by August of that year. The job description was for an audio program developer, which I assumed meant a close alignment with my radio background. I was wrong.

As weeks passed I realized there was no need for my position; I had almost nothing to do and begged the director to move me elsewhere—perhaps television production where personnel were overburdened with assignments, but he refused, insisting that I concentrate on how to best produce and utilize audio in the college classrooms. To initiate the process, he sent me on a tour of other state schools to see what audio programmers were developing on those campuses.

The excursion took me throughout New York State, where I viewed historic sites such as Underground Railroad stopping points, George Washington slept here taverns, and historic forts, in addition to the requisite college campuses. I learned that none of the other institutions had a job description similar to mine, and I reported this to my supervisor, who remained undeterred. "Something will come up," he said. "Stay with it."

I finally managed a program—a pronunciation guide for the campus speech therapist—for which the therapist generously gave me credit on the paper he placed in a professional journal reporting on how to incorporate the guide into therapy sessions.

Other than that I maintained morale in the department by arriving for work thirty minutes later than my colleagues, and spending another half-hour perusing mail or responding to very infrequent phone messages. Then I would head up the hallway lined with staff offices and begin with the first one. We'd adjourn to a campus cafeteria for coffee. Twenty minutes later we'd return, and I'd accompany the occupant of the next office for his coffee. This continued until thirty minutes before lunch, each professional staffer joining me for morning coffee. Following lunch, I'd visit the campus library and peruse magazines and newspapers to which I aspired to contribute. Then began a repeat of the morning routine, and I had afternoon coffee with colleagues until the workday ended.

When I complained about having nothing to do, acquaintances and friends urged me to count my blessings; where else could I receive $11,000 a year for having coffee and reading in the library?

I finally decided to bring my writing projects to the office and while away hours with those. Our department head seemed unconcerned that I wasn't developing more audio projects, so I continued alternating writing with providing coffee break companionship to the rest of the staff.

One afternoon, Judy returned from an outing with the college faculty wives. They had visited a unique little museum in tiny Chazy, New York, just up the interstate, and a few miles south of the border with Quebec. The museum was founded by William H. Miner, a native son who made a fortune by inventing the railroad car coupling, and who was a friend of Thomas Edison. Miner had endowed a number of North Country institutions, including the high school in Chazy, in which he installed one of the first school swimming pools in the country.

Miner also paid for the new surgical wing at the hospital in Plattsburgh and insisted on being its first patient. He was sixty-seven then, in excellent health, and doctors attempted to dissuade him. Something simple, he insisted; a tonsillectomy should be no problem. It was done, but complications arose, and Miner died.

His museum was not limited to, but centered its collection on the Revolutionary War period, holding letters from George Washington and a musket belonging to Benedict Arnold. There was cutlery from Andrew Jackson's Hermitage and other presidential items belonging to William McKinley and Abraham Lincoln. The collection was remarkable, even more so because it was located in out of the way Chazy.

Judy gave an enthusiastic report on the museum and suggested I pay a visit and write about it. I did, and spent a delightful afternoon with the museum's curator, who, ignoring the "Do Not Touch" signs, often grabbed objects, thrusting them into my hands. I was most awed by hefting for several seconds a walking stick that had belonged to Lincoln.

Returning home I wrote a 700-word piece that I sent to travel editors of newspapers in Albany and Syracuse, hoping one of them might buy it for $50 or so. When neither did, Judy insisted I send it to *The New York Times*.

"If papers in Albany and Syracuse refused it, why in the world do you think the *Times* would be interested?"

"Because it's a *New York Times* story," she said. "You send it to them."

I knew better, so I didn't until the next week when she saw the manuscript still on my desk. "If you don't mail it, I'll do it myself," she said.

I gave in and off it went.

In those days in the village of Peru where we lived, residents picked up mail at the post office. I used to stop by on my way to work, and ten days after mailing the story to the *Times*, I found the return envelope in my box. Through the envelope I could feel the cardboard I'd used to keep photos from bending during mailing. It was, I knew, the expected rejection. I almost chucked the envelope in the trash, but took it to the car, where I opened it.

The photos I submitted were there, but the manuscript wasn't. It was Thursday and I was wondrously astonished to see a tear sheet from next Sunday's travel page with my article. The photos I'd submitted didn't pass muster, and the paper printed a couple of file shots of museum artifacts, but the brief note said I'd be paid $150 for the story.

Instead of motoring on to work, I returned home where Judy and I danced about our spare living room and planned a big night out in Montreal.

This was in 1970, and it remains to this day my most cherished acceptance—in large part stemming from how surprised I was with the news that I'd scored with the venerable *New York Times* on my first attempt.

Shortly after the Miner Museum story appeared in the *Times*, the Peabody Maritime Museum in Salem, Massachusetts phoned. Its public relations director wanted me to come to Salem, look at the facility, and see if I could get a piece on it in the *Times* travel pages, too. They'd pick up all my expenses.

As a relative neophyte I didn't know accepting gratuities was inappropriate, so I agreed to visit Salem, where Nathaniel Hawthorne's *House of Seven Gables* and The Salem Witch House are also located.

After spending a morning at the Peabody, I devoted the afternoon to those other sites and wrote a Salem story, which the *Times* rejected, but both the *Chicago Sun-Times* and *Los Angeles Times* printed. While *The New York Times* insisted on exclusive rights to a story, most other papers were satisfied with regional rights, assuming that residents in Chicago were not subscribers to Los Angeles papers, and vice-versa.

Additionally, a restructured feature on the Peabody sold to a magazine called *Sailing*. *The New York Times* rejection was fortuitous; the three sales brought $220—$70 more than the *Times* would have paid for exclusive rights. A year later a veteran travel writer told me I'd committed an ethical error in accepting expenses from the Peabody, and I've never again breached that protocol.

In June of 1970, while visiting Judy's family in Spooner, Wisconsin, I spent a day in nearby Hayward, "The Muskie Capital of the World." I visited with resort owners, muskie aficionados, and small business owners, attempting to get a handle on what the legendary, toothsome pike meant to the local economy. I envisioned a business-oriented article, but upon returning to our Peru, NY home, and pecking away at the old Royal manual typewriter, I found I'd written a travel piece written instead. The *Times* travel editor agreed, and ran that one too. I'd placed two travel pieces in the *Times* within six months.

I've often thought about those initial sales to *The New York Times*, especially the first one. I was astonished that the *Times* would take a piece that smaller, far less prestigious papers had rejected.

Yet stranger things can happen in a writing career. In May of 1988 I participated in a "Writes of Spring" workshop at the University of Wisconsin-Stevens Point. Other participants included Terry McMillan before she published her bestseller *Waiting to Exhale,* and *The New Yorker* writer Alec Wilkinson. Over dinner one night Wilkinson said that when he graduated from Bennington College, he worked for a year as a police officer in his Massachusetts hometown, before seeking a job in journalism. He carried clips and resumes to many regional daily newspapers and also small-town weeklies. All of them declined his application.

Deciding he had nothing to lose, he ventured into New York City and applied at dailies there. More turn-downs. Then he passed the building housing *The New Yorker* magazine. On a whim he entered the office, and with the same clips and resume applied for a job and was immediately hired. Apparently not qualified to work at far lesser publications, Wilkinson had just the right stuff for *The New Yorker,* and he has been a mainstay there for more than thirty years.

CHAPTER 7

STRINGING ALONG:
The Christian Science Monitor
and *The New York Times*

OLLOWING THE MINER MUSEUM STORY, MY STANDING ON THE
Plattsburg campus ascended. Our dean was delighted to take me to
lunches at the local Rotary, Lions, Optimist, and Kiwanis clubs, where I
was introduced as a young faculty member who wrote for *The New York Times*.
Not pressured to try and develop audio programs, I was asked what projects I
might enjoy working on. For several weeks I filled in directing some television
segments and writing a department brochure.

(An aside: I participated in an anti-Vietnam war march in downtown
Plattsburgh one Saturday morning. I didn't fear losing my job here, as I was
already considering moving elsewhere anyway. I truly had nothing to worry
about, however, because upon falling in with other marchers on that chilly but
sunny day, I found myself next to the dean who oversaw our department.)

By the time the muskie story appeared in the *Times*, I'd begun looking for
another job. It just didn't feel right to collect a full-time paycheck while only
performing part-time tasks. I suppose I might have gone on indefinitely, letting campus bigwigs cart me off to lunches and banquets because I'd written
for *The New York Times*, but the puritan in me couldn't justify pay for so little
work, and when a job teaching lower division speech classes at North Hennepin

Community College in Brooklyn Park, Minnesota opened in the summer of 1970, I applied and was hired.

By then I'd sold more than a dozen articles to *The Christian Science Monitor*, and after settling in on the campus, and determining that even with a full teaching load there remained ample time for writing, I contacted the *Monitor* about becoming their Twin Cities stringer. Stringers are employed by major newspapers and broadcast outlets (and now news oriented websites) to cover regions where these operations don't have news bureaus. The stringer is a freelance reporter who is paid per assignment to send stories or information upon request to the paper or network. The term stringer comes from the old weekly small town papers that hired area residents to submit news from their neighborhoods to the paper. These contributors would clip their articles and "string" them together to submit for payment at the end of the month. Typically the rural weeklies paid (and may still pay) about ten cents per column inch—an inch typically is between thirty and forty words, depending on print font.

An aside: a Plattsburgh colleague who subscribed to his hometown Danemora, NY weekly, cheekily argued that the only real news was in those rural papers with stories about Mrs. Elwood Kinsley's bean supper, and the Calvin Edmonson's 500-card party, attended by three other couples, and what a grand time they had. "Everybody knows the goings on in Washington, London, New York, and other major cities in the world," my friend said. "But until appearing in the Danemora paper, nobody would have known about the Edmonson's 500 party."

Those and similar events were "news" in small towns across America, and stringers often padded their pieces with names of all attendees and detailed recipes for each hors d'oeuvres served to guests. Often these extraneous entries were excised, but during weeks when space was available, they might be included, and perhaps a stringer earned fifty cents or a dollar more that week.

Large newspapers, however, don't pay by the column inch, but on a per assignment basis, and I would come to have that arrangement with both *The Christian Science Monitor*, *The New York Times*, and briefly with *Business Week Magazine*.

Guy Halverson, the *Monitor's* Chicago bureau chief, gave me free reign to contact him with story ideas, and he in turn sent suggestions that I might develop. It became a fruitful relationship over the next five years as I not only wrote news features for the *Monitor,* but also contributed nearly a dozen "Focus" columns for the paper during the early 1970s. "Focus" appeared on the front page and as explained by Halverson, columns were not hard news driven, but breezier, lighter pieces running about 650 words. I wrote about zoos, prison reform, and educational innovations among sundry other subjects for "Focus." Once I had both a "Focus" column and another news feature appear on the *Monitor* front page, and Halverson phoned me. "You're the first stringer to get two stories on the same front page," he said. "You may not know it, but our reporters are competitive and covet that front page. It's unheard of for a stringer, and even unlikely for a regular reporter to have two front page stories in the same edition."

Writing for the *Monitor* I learned how to peg pieces, even the hard news articles. *Monitor* stories, Halverson told me, needed to have "legs"—that is, they had to be newsworthy a week or so later because many subscribers received the paper in the mail several days following publication.

By 1975, however, Guy Halverson was moved from Chicago. His replacement and I didn't hit it off nearly so well, and that affiliation lapsed.

At the same time, however, I started writing more travel articles, all of which the *Times* rejected, but were subsequently placed in the *Chicago Sun-Times,* the *Los Angeles Times, Newsday,* and elsewhere. I was learning that a newspaper travel writer didn't need to journey very far to churn out saleable stories. I wrote about an outsider sculptor in Phillips, Wisconsin, 90 miles from my home. Another Wisconsinite made life-sized woodcarvings of Biblical figures in Spooner, my wife's hometown. I also wrote about Charles Lindberg's boyhood home in Little Falls, Minnesota, Sinclair Lewis's boyhood home in Sauk Centre, and F. Scott Fitzgerald's St. Paul house where he finished the manuscript for *This Side of Paradise.* I wrote about the Minnesota Iron Range's Callithumpian parade on the Fourth of July, and mined other locales that were just a short hop away. It took a couple years before these sources were exhausted.

And when they were, I taught a travel writing course at The Loft Literary Center in Minneapolis, and offered a travel writing tip: there are travel stories to be written about well-known destinations that haven't been written yet. Go to Disneyland or Disneyworld and write a story about some behind the scenes goings on, like the first aid station or police operations.

A few students took me up on this suggestion and managed to produce first sales, which is rewarding for a teacher to have fostered.

While I was in a bit of a writer's drought myself, it ended when I began regularly contributing features to a magazine titled *American Education*, a publication of the U. S. Department of Education, that paid $300 per accepted article. William A. Horn was managing editor, and I sent him a query suggesting an article about a program on our campus that brought older students seeking new careers to classes designed to help them meet their goals. Horn wasn't much interested, but said if I wanted to go ahead and write the piece on speculation, he would have a look. Turned out he liked it and sent me $300 with an offer to send him more stories. I don't recall my second pitch, but once more he sent a half-hearted response saying if I insisted, he'd at least read the piece. Again, he sent another check, and this time told me that so long as federal dollars were involved with unique programs in education, he'd commission almost anything I'd suggest in the future. One was a widely-circulated article about the vocational school in Staples, Minnesota, titled, "The School that Saved a Town." Classes in heavy equipment operation there constructed the local airport, among other projects the city couldn't afford, and its agriculture department secured contracts for area farmers to produce cucumbers for Gedney Pickles.

In 1973 I earned enough from Horn's journal and a few other markets to allow Judy and me to spend three weeks in the British Isles, Ireland, and France. In addition we purchased a used car and a dining room suite that is still in use on my freelance income of around $5,000 that year. It tells you something about the decline of the dollar's value over the decades.

By the late seventies, Horn had retired, and a year or so following his retirement the publication folded.

It would not be easy to replace the $1,500 to $1,800 annual income I'd been receiving from Bill Horn, and my writing output sagged until I connected with *The New York Times* as its Minnesota stringer.

Since Minnesota was a hub for medical advancements, with the Mayo Clinic based in Rochester, and the emerging work done at the University of Minnesota Hospitals, I envisioned numerous health-related articles. The *Monitor*, however, would not have been interested, and indeed, could not run stories about medical technology and new research. I began to shift allegiance from the *Monitor* to the *Times*, which accelerated after Halverson moved from Chicago.

I approached the *Times* about stringing for them, informing the news department about my travel pieces, and sending them clips from the *Monitor*. A week or so later a letter arrived from Irv Horowitz of the New York news bureau. I would be given routine assignments from that department, mostly consisting of conducting local interviews for national roundup stories, and preparing memos for the reporters assigned to write them. I submitted data on milk prices, divorce laws, traffic issues, regional politics—myriad topics about some of which I knew little and others which held scant interest for me. I was, however, paid from $35 to $60 for each memo.

But none of that required any writing, per se; I functioned like a research assistant, gathering quotes and data and submitting them. However, there was a definite cachet in being associated with *The New York Times*. I was routinely invited to plant openings and soirees by corporate executives who were interested in getting America's newspaper of record to consider their programs to improve employee morale, or in the case of nonprofits, how they expanded their services.

The downside was that stringers, even if they contributed a complete story, did not receive bylines in the news section of the paper. But I did once. It was back in 1978, when President Jimmy Carter initiated conferences on the American family in several regional locales around the country. Minneapolis was one of them.

The *Times* reporter assigned to cover the Minneapolis conclave became ill and the news desk asked if I could fill in during the two-day event. I filed a report on the first day, and was surprised to see my nearly unedited article in the next day's paper, complete with my byline. Horowitz phoned saying it had been a mistake, and my next report would be published sans the byline. My compensation was a $300 check for two days work.

It was during the *Times* tenure, which lasted nearly fifteen years, that I became acutely aware of the paper's power. Inevitably when I'd phone a politician, civic leader, or business executive and say I was representing *The New York Times*, I could almost hear a gasp on the other end, and sense the genuflecting pause as the reality set in. "My god, it's *The NEW YORK TIMES!*"

I utilized my stringer status at the paper to secure some freelance assignments, mostly from the Sunday Financial pages, where I profiled area entrepreneurs, corporations, and executives.

However esteemed the *Times* was/is, its personnel were very human and not necessarily as knowledgeable as outsiders might assume. Once I wrote an article about the old Control Data Corporation and mentioned a policy there that enabled the company to significantly reduce its Workman's Compensation (now Workers' Compensation) costs. It wasn't a major part of the story, and I gave it only one sentence in the 1,000-word submission.

The day after I filed the story, an assistant editor from the financial section phoned. "Here on the second page, you mention Workman's Compensation," he said.

"Yes," I said.

"That's not enough," he said.

"What do you mean?"

"You just put it out there without explaining what it is."

"I didn't think readers of the business pages in the *Times* needed an explanation."

His voice turned cranky. "Send a paragraph that tells me about this Workman's Compensation. Is this a government program? Get me the details."

Pause. "I really don't think—"

"Just do it," he snapped.

"Okay," I said, not wanting to jeopardize any future assignments, but astonished that a business editor with the *Times* didn't know what Workman's Compensation was.

I dutifully put together a detailed definition for the assistant editor and phoned it in. But I felt embarrassed because if the piece appeared in print, the explanation might seem under the heads of *Times* readers, who would surely comprehend the program.

When the piece was published the following Sunday, the Workman's Comp explanation was absent, and I theorized that someone else in the department—likely Colleen Sullivan who commissioned the article—caught it and eliminated that excess from the final copy.

During my first few years of writing for the *Times*, freelancers were not required to sign "work made for hire" agreements. A work for hire arrangement is a long-established practice among media, and it means that if you're employed by a newspaper or a radio or television station, the work you do for them is theirs and belongs to them. Most freelance writers, however, were free to resell their writing elsewhere, giving credit to the original publishers of the stories or articles. It was understood that material freelancers sold to the *Times* belonged to the *Times* for first North American publication only; we contributors assumed that we'd split future sales of our work with the publisher if they generated reprinting, and the profit would be entirely ours if we managed to place it.

I'd written an article about how the Control Data Corporation had established a bindery in a downtrodden area of Minneapolis in order to provide employment to local residents. The story generated a lot of discussion about social responsibility of large corporations.

While developing that story, I interviewed William Norris, Control Data founder and CEO. About five minutes into the session, four security officers burst into his office, asking the startled Norris if everything was okay, casting suspicious glances my way. Norris assured them there was no problem, then, grinning sheepishly, turned to me. "I inadvertently hit this button here which tells security there's trouble." He sighed. "This new technology is moving too fast for me, I guess."

This from a man who played a major role in catapulting the culture into the computer age, and who, apparently, didn't quite comprehend his own desktop apparatus.

However, a year later, while back at Control Data pursuing another story, a corporate vice president passed me in the hall. After a brief exchange, he said he'd been pleased to see the original story reprinted in a United States Information Agency publication. That magazine circulated only in Europe and Asia, and there was virtually no chance I'd ever see the story. I contacted the *Times*, and to their credit they cut a check for $100.

That story came to the attention of a professor at the University of Minnesota, who was teaching a graduate course in business management. He encouraged his students, nearly all of whom were employed and working on their graduate degrees part-time, to read it. One of these students was a textbook salesman who visited my office at the community college one or two times each year.

Those of us teaching lower division courses knew we were not much esteemed by faculties at four-year state colleges and universities. Our teaching loads were about sixteen hours per week, while full professors seldom taught more than nine hours per week. We did grunt work; they siphoned off the cream upper-class and graduate pupils.

My textbook salesman reported to me that he told the class he knew the author of the article, an instructor at North Hennepin, to which his professor exclaimed, "That's not possible," as if a Harvard doctorate were a prerequisite for publishing anything in the Sunday *New York Times*.

About midway through my *Times'* tenure, the paper insisted that each published piece in the paper was "work made for hire," and by endorsing the checks for article payment, we contributors supposedly agreed to those terms. Many corporations utilize a similar policy with employees who invent or modify processes on company time. The company gets the patent.

I didn't agree with the *Times* new injunction, but neither did I protest; I simply lined out the "work for hire" statement on checks, and initialed them, figuring no one would notice. I later resold a couple of those pieces, and as I guessed no one from the *Times* complained.

Though often sought by local corporations and public relations operatives to pitch potential stories to the *Times,* I only followed through once. The flamboyant Percy Ross had made millions by recycling resins and coloring them black, then manufacturing plastic garbage bags at a far lower cost than bag makers who used virgin resins which were clear.

But that wasn't the story I would write. Ross was fiercely ego-driven and craved attention from the press and public. He'd been receiving a lot of publicity by contributing gifts to the underprivileged (1,000 bicycles for kids from struggling families), buying groceries for food shelves, paying for expensive surgeries, and making tuition payments for students. Whenever his benevolence struck, it did so with requisite media attention; it was his obsession, the string he attached to his charity. No television and newspaper coverage, no gift.

I found all this quite fascinating and pitched the profile to Colleen Sullivan. She also was intrigued, but said that there had to be a news peg on which to hang the piece.

I mentioned the possibility of *The New York Times* being interested in a profile, and asked Ross if he'd be available for an interview. He was, and invited me to his office, which was festooned with gorgeous young women who could have been fashion models or Hollywood starlets. Ross's office facility in Bloomington was James Bondish. In the hallway from his office to a meeting room, he paused and nodded at a framed abstract painting on the wall. "Very nice," I said absently.

"Look here," he said, moving the painting and voila! The wall opened into a small cabaret, replete with well-stocked bar and bandstand. "Salesmen and others come calling," Ross said. "If I'm going to be tied up, I send them in here and soften them up before we deal. Of course sometimes there's a party, and even with music you can't hear it in the rest of the building."

As we sat in his office, whenever the phone rang, he put it on speaker, desiring I listen in. I'm not sure why he did this, but I was dazzled by the female pulchritude and the bling that featured gold-plated fixtures in the rest rooms and television sets in the showers. But, I told Ross, there was no story unless it could attach itself to a news peg.

His face fell for a moment, but he said, "I think we'll be able to fix that."

And the next day he called and said the Treasury Department was going to sell a million dollars' worth of highly collectable Morgan silver dollars. "I've made an offer to buy the entire stock," he said, "and donate them to a bunch of charities. There's your news peg."

Ross was right; he knew his bid would be refused, and it was, but he also understood it would be headline copy. In New York, Colleen Sullivan agreed, and I wrote the story, which upon publication created a sensation. If the story had appeared in the Internet age, it would have gone viral. The Percy Ross article was reprinted around the world. Ross showed me copies in at least a half-dozen languages including Chinese and Hebrew. He was delighted with his new international celebrity.

He had to hire another comely lass to answer the phone inquiries generated by that piece, and when callers failed to get through to Ross, they'd call me with their schemes to get Ross publicity for participating in their special ventures.

Following *Times* publication, Percy Ross toyed with syndicating a television show in which people pleading righteous causes competed with each other for securing a large sum of money from him. This never came to fruition, but in today's "reality" TV crazed culture, it would surely thrive.

But Ross did parlay the publicity into a nationally syndicated newspaper column, "Thanks a Million," in which he invited readers to share their sob stories or favorite charity needs. He published their letters along with his responses—often reasons why the request was not met. "Thanks A Million" also became a syndicated radio program running on four hundred stations across the country. It was Ross's stated goal to give away his vast fortune before he died. By his own estimation he succeeded, and said he'd donated an unverified $30 million by 1999 when his mission ended. Ross died in 2001, but a touch of his fame rubbed off on me. For years following the *Times* story about Ross, people called or wrote to ask me to comment about him, including writers who wanted to find something unseemly about him. His generosity was legitimate, I always said, but the man was possessed of a monstrous ego.

It certainly never bothered me that he expected a ton of publicity for his charity. And what about others' reactions? Ask any of those thousand kids who got bicycles from him if they resented all the newspaper photos and television clips that accompanied the Percy Ross gifts.

CHAPTER 8

BREAKING INTO BOOKS

I N 1974 I JOINED AMICUS, INC. THIS WAS AN ORGANIZATION FOUNDED by a Minneapolis judge, Neil Reilly, who during his lengthy tenure on the bench had witnessed too many felons returning again and again to his court for sentencing on new crimes. Why can't these guys get it together and go straight? Reilly often wondered.

Finally, he sought answers, and chief among them was that when cons get released from their sentences, the only people they know, or who will associate with them, are other ex-cons. One thing leads to another, and often within a year of release many felons are sent back to prison for parole violations or for committing new offenses.

Reilly's thrust behind Amicus was to recruit men who'd never been convicted of anything and ask them to befriend a man in the Minnesota State Prison at Stillwater. He secured a staff to run the operation, and a non-offender would be paired with a con—usually based on mutual interests, the theory being that the soon to be released convict has at least one straight friend he can talk to on the outside.

By the time I volunteered, the organization had begun establishing some impressive statistics. A con with an Amicus buddy was indeed less likely to recidivate.

During my Amicus association, I befriended two cons, Mel and Barney, over a five-year period. Mel was habituated to life in the joint and never made a successful adjustment—inability to avoid alcohol being his downfall. Barney, a stick-up guy, also had a weakness for booze, but he eventually avoided re-incarceration, not because he wouldn't re-offend, but because in his own words, "I've gotten too damn old for that game. I couldn't even run across the street anymore." He wrote two books on his prison experiences, and writing and publishing was the center of our relationship. At the time Barney was more widely published than I, and I anticipated his imparting useful pointers during our monthly sessions. He was entirely intuitive about his work, however, and only told me to "Study the markets and see what they want. Then give it to them."

Easier said than done, of course, but Barney, who wrote mostly for children's Sunday school papers, seldom earning more than two cents per word, nonetheless lived well for an inmate. His writing income enabled him to have a radio and television set in his cell, a small refrigerator and an electric coffee pot.

As I became more involved with Amicus, it seemed natural that I should write about the program, and I published articles in *The Christian Science Monitor* and the Jesuit magazine *America* about the organization. Soon other publications sought Amicus stories, and I think I wrote two more.

During one of these later assignments, I met Ted Jefferson, who had served time for manslaughter and had, with the help of his Amicus friend, turned his life around.

When I met Ted, he was running a street ministry and a halfway house for newly released convicts. Raised on the mean streets of Milwaukee, Ted began running afoul of the law while still in elementary school, stealing bicycles. He moved along the ladder to shoplifting, pimping, drug running—the clichéd inner city lifestyle of young black men in America.

Finally, he shot and killed a man in a Minneapolis after-hours establishment. He was three months on the lamb before being captured in Detroit. For reasons he never understood, he was able to plead guilty to manslaughter instead of murder, and served seven years in the penitentiary.

While incarcerated, however, he experienced a religious conversion and became active in penal Christian circles, serving as chaplain's assistant, and earning the trust of prison officials who recommended him for early release.

Though I was interviewing him for a magazine story, I thought this guy's life should be in a book. Ted agreed and over the next year we worked together on a manuscript published first by Masters Press, and later in paperback by Baker Book House, titled *One Bad Dude.*

Judy and I celebrated its publication with a Sunday brunch at a local hotel with friends. Masters even came through with a modest advance that Ted and I split. *One Bad Dude* appeared early in 1978, and Ted deservedly got a lot of attention for it, appearing on many leading Christian media outlets, including Jim and Tammy Faye Bakker's PTL Club and Pat Robertson's 700 Club. He was impressed with the first-class accommodations provided him by the Bakkers, but the visit troubled him. He reported that he'd witnessed some of the peccadilloes that later surfaced in press reports and brought about the end of the PTL Club and a prison sentence for Jim Bakker.

Ted suffered a heart attack and died shy of his sixtieth birthday in the mid-1980s.

Near the end of my association with the *Times* I'd grown bored with gathering quotes and statistical data and arranging them as memos for other reporters. Also, Colleen Sullivan had moved on (apparently deeply depressed, she committed suicide at age forty, several years later), and I was having no luck pitching future pieces to her replacement.

During this same time span, I began writing for Sunday supplement sections in other daily newspapers. I profiled football legend Bronko Nagurski for the supplements in the *Chicago Sun-Times* and the *St. Paul Pioneer Press.* I wrote an education feature for the nationally circulated *Parade* magazine, and even hit *Reader's Digest* a decade and a half after that initial attempt. This time, I wrote about a local man, Tom McDonald, a perennial office-seeker in both Minneapolis and at the state level, who was not taken seriously by voters, but who had a heart for the downtrodden. He solicited an army of volunteers who would perform services for the financially troubled, like fixing their cars, purchasing groceries, or even providing temporary shelter. The story ran in a department called "Involved Americans," but I did not get the coveted $1,000 for it.

Apparently my story needed extensive editing to "read" more like a *Digest* piece. I was paid $500, and the co-author from the magazine came to Minneapolis where he treated McDonald, his wife, and Judy and me to an expensive dinner at the legendary but no-longer- in-existence downtown diner, Charlie's Café Exceptionale.

In the meantime, along with millions of Americans, I was caught up in the fitness craze: long distance running. And since I was running races from five kilometers to the marathon, I figured why not write about running.

A local young man, Dick Beardsley, was beginning to achieve national attention as a marathoner, and had recently set the record for the Grandma's Marathon course in Duluth, Minnesota—a record that lasted more than thirty years. I approached *Runner's World* magazine about profiling Dick for them. They gave me the assignment on speculation. I wrote it anyway, and they bought it, thus beginning a five-year relationship with the magazine that eventually put my name on the masthead as Midwest Editor, and later as Contributing Editor.

Regarding the former, I edited nothing but my own copy, as I submitted features and news on the Minnesota running scene. I did the same as contributing editor, and it was a profitable arrangement. I was publishing four to six articles each year for between $400 and $600 each, depending on length.

Many pieces I wrote for *Runner's World* were about diet and health, co-written with physicians, chiropractors, and nutritionists. It occurred to me that I might expand this health and fitness work to local radio. I came up with a format for a weekly five-minute presentation on health and fitness tips. The first station I approached was KSTP-AM in St. Paul. A meeting was arranged with a producer, and I arrived early for my appointment.

I waited in a large atrium ringed by offices, perusing a magazine until the producer could see me. After sitting several minutes I heard voices and heels clicking on the highly polished floor. I looked up and saw two men walking toward me, immediately noticing one of the men, Stanley Hubbard, owner of that station and many others around the country. I think I audibly gasped upon recognizing the man with him: legendary screen actor Jimmy Stewart, then in his mid-seventies, but still a strikingly handsome man with silver hair, wearing a tailored navy pin-striped suit. He must have seen the look on my face for he paused momentarily in front of me and said in that almost clichéd, time-worn Jimmy Stewart manner, "H-How ya doin?" before continuing on his way. I don't think I verbally responded, but mouth agape, nodded.

The KSTP fellow liked my idea, but it fell through at a meeting with others who ultimately decide those things, and I connected instead with that station's rival Twin Cities radio giant, WCCO-AM, which gave me a five-minute segment on Sunday mornings. The feature aired for a little over a year. It was the only time the broadcast major figured in my career. The pieces were fun; sometimes an essay, other broadcasts had me interviewed by the program host. I was paid $25 per program at first, but at the end I was receiving $50. I was also hired by the station as an on-the-scene reporter for the first two Twin Cities Marathons, covering the masters' competitions among runners over age forty, both male and female.

Back in 1973 I considered writing a novel. For reasons I no longer recall, I decided to set the story in northern Minnesota in the aftermath of World War 1.

Pondering the novel, I remembered a comment my mother had made when I was perhaps nine or ten years old. She'd said that when she was a little girl a large mob, estimated at between 5,000 and 10,000 men, women, and children formed in downtown Duluth, broke into the jail, and hanged three young black men. It happened on June 15, 1920, and I later learned that the mob victims had been accused of raping a local white girl, though the accusations would later prove false.

I cannot recall the context of Mother's remark, but the incident surfaced as I contemplated my novel. I'd never heard any mention of a Duluth lynching after that, except a playmate's father, in whose garage print shop we often hung out to warm ourselves during cold winter afternoons, once replied to my query about the tragedy that a lot of folks weren't sure the girl alleged to have been attacked by the three men—employees of a traveling circus—had actually been assaulted.

Mr. Hassinger's comment was likely stated during the school Christmas break in 1949—twenty-nine years after the lynchings.

Because it seemed very few knew or had heard about the killings, I thought it would make an interesting chapter in my novel. My main character would be an eye witness to the incident, and since I wanted to be as accurate as possible, I sought the book I assumed someone had written about those lynchings fifty or so years earlier. But there was no such book. Further, librarians in and around Duluth had never heard of this incident. Neither had other librarians and historians throughout northern Minnesota.

How could this be? The incident must have been widely publicized at the time. Yet nobody knew anything about it?

Several months later, an archivist at the Minnesota Historical Society in St. Paul called and said he'd discovered a small folder on the lynchings, which would be available to me.

There wasn't much there: just a photo of the lynch tableau that had been made into postcards, and a short pamphlet describing the killings. I quickly began poring over newspapers from the era, and within two Saturday sessions at the Historical Society library, I had filled a Spiral notebook with data and information regarding the lynchings.

At some point around 1975, I decided to abandon my novel, which wasn't progressing, and instead concentrate on documenting this significant but long-forgotten tragedy. It would take fifteen months to complete my research, relying mostly on old newspaper accounts, and also interviews with local persons who were somehow connected to the incident. Few were actual eye witnesses, though one man claimed to be, and I was excited to interview someone who had actually been present, and who said he was near the jail as it was broken into, and had seen all three victims dragged up the hill one block and hanged from a lamp post.

We met at a downtown Duluth bakery and coffee shop, and I turned on my reel-to-reel tape recorder. The man's recall seemed vivid and rich as he told me about conversations he overheard regarding what was about to happen. He claimed he saw men with new rope emerge from a hardware store across the street, and the victims, at least one of whom had soiled himself, being dragged out and beaten by the mob before one by one they were strung upon the corner lamp post and killed. I immediately began to transcribe the tape upon my return home.

But something was wrong, which led me to believe the man was a wannabe, and his story was false. Less than two minutes into the recording this fellow reported that after work that day, he had met a friend at a tavern two doors down from the police station, where they drank beer until the fracas was underway.

What was wrong with this man's depiction? The year was 1920 and the Volstead Act—Prohibition—was in force. There were no taverns or speakeasies on Superior Street, the main artery of Duluth's downtown, and one certainly wouldn't have been situated two doors away from law enforcement headquarters. While there were scattered speakeasies at that time, they were across the St. Louis River in Superior, Wisconsin.

As soon as I listened to his story again, I realized I could not, in good conscience, use any of his anecdotes in assembling an account of the lynchings, and had to rely on more prosaic descriptions, not from actual eyewitnesses, but from descendants of eye witnesses, and second-hand accounts from Duluthians not directly involved.

Though I'd written articles for both newspapers and magazines at that time, I'd never done any investigative work, and was quite naive in my approach. Several sources, whose stories I thought necessary, said they would decline to be interviewed unless I agreed to change the names of the alleged rape victim and her escort on that night.

A tough-minded journalist would never agree to this, but I acquiesced, thinking I needed cooperation from these folks, so created aliases for Irene Tusken, who became Sandra Teale in the original text, and for James Sullivan, who was assigned Robert Walsh. I regret having done this, but through the years, as more people have become aware of the lynchings, the true identities have been often published elsewhere. (The subjects were correctly identified in the second edition of *The Lynchings in Duluth,* released in 2016.)

I spent a year writing and rewriting the manuscript, and because this incident had been forgotten, I assumed there would be significant interest in the story.

But more than thirty publishers passed on the manuscript over the next three-and-a-half years. One, the Minnesota Historical Society Press, was regionally chauvinistic back then, and some officers of the society were displeased that I would try to publish something unseemly about the state. And the book was ignored by all society publications following its appearance. However, during the submission period, several editors commented on the book, articulating their refusal. Two of those responses seemed astonishingly politically incorrect, even for the late 1970s. One editor said he thought I'd done a good job with the text but could not "profitably publish this manuscript because black people don't read books." Another said publication could instigate riots, resulting in injuries and property damage.

Agents who saw the manuscript had similar responses; they didn't think mainstream publishers would be intrigued by a half-century-old crime that happened in Duluth because civil rights books had become, in their word, "passé." This was before *Roots* became a runaway best-seller.

Finally, in June 1978, a small Orange County, California publisher, Brasch and Brasch, took the manuscript and titled it *They Was Just Niggers.* The unseemly title came from a quote issued by a Duluth resident upon learning that martial law had been declared in the city. "Why all the fuss?" he mused. "After all, they was just niggers."

I was delighted to place the work but was unaware of potential problems publishing with a small, neophyte independent press. I suppose I was in league with many other writers of a first book who, eager for acceptance and publication, may, after a dozen or so rejections from major houses, jump at the opportunity to place his work with a small independent publisher. While this gets his name on a cover, it is not necessarily a consummation devoutly to be wished. Or it wasn't in the case of my book, which appeared in May 1979.

By all accounts that initial edition of the book was a critical success but a marketplace fizzle. About two years following publication, I think I understood why.

Publisher Walter Brasch was trying to get his fledging firm off the ground. His operation would rapidly expand, he said, and my book was just what he was looking for to help establish credibility for his company.

Four months following Brasch's acceptance of the book, Robert Smith, a *Minneapolis Tribune* columnist, heard of my work and wrote a story, prompting other papers and a regional magazine to inquire about excerpting chapters. Publication date was November. The ball was rolling.

November came and went. Brasch said printing bids had come in over budget and he hoped to get a better deal. The book would not materialize until mid-May.

By the time the book appeared, whatever clamor was generated by excerpts in the newspaper and magazines had diminished. Still, the book was ordered by a few stores in the Midwest and California. But Brasch didn't wish to relinquish 40 to 45% of the list price to a distributor and undertook this task himself, placing inordinate trust in the U. S. Postal Service. I'm aware of at least 150 ordered books never reaching bookstores.

Brasch quickly learned of another substantial problem. Large book divisions in major chains won't order just one title from a small company. A small press title with a respected distributor stands a much better chance of finding its way into stores.

But I wasn't unduly concerned. I still basked in the euphoria of publication. Several media appearances had already been scheduled in the Midwest; my picture appeared in our local weekly, and my youngest daughter announced to her first-grade class that her father was a famous author and would soon be rich. We would be moving to a big new house with a swimming pool. Throwing caution to the winds, I purchased two retreads for our 1968 Dodge.

Then on Sunday, June 24, Brasch phoned, his voice crackling with excitement. "You made the *L.A. Times*," he said, and read the brief though laudatory assessment in the "Notable" section of those pages. "That's a start," he said. "We're on our way."

Other strong reviews followed. Four stars from the *West Coast Review of Books*. A reviewer for Minnesota Public Radio compared the book to *Invitation to a Lynching*, which won a Pulitzer Prize. Major reviews in appeared the *Milwaukee Journal*, the *San Francisco Review of Books,* and even the Spooner, Wisconsin *Advocate.*

But we weren't on our way. Despite those reviews, virtually nothing happened, for reviews—even raves—don't sell many books. They do not sell books because bookstore buyers are not influenced by them. According to Kay Sexton, former president of the old B. Dalton bookstore chain, "A mention in *Publishers Weekly* may resonate with booksellers, but what really grabs them is a substantial advertising budget. That gets the author posters and front table displays."

Of course, my book had neither posters nor front table placement as Brasch's advertising budget was minimal. My book, with other midlist releases, appeared in category shelves, and could be found in Regional or Sociology sections. The stark cover of the lynch tableau—a postcard in 1920—was not visible.

Even among those stores ordering books, Brasch encountered problems. In at least three instances, stores never paid for books ordered and presumably sold. At one store, more than one hundred paperback copies were sold, representing about $60 in royalties for me. That $60 equaled the cost of the retreads on my old car. A small publisher may not have the clout to require prompt payment.

A case also might be made that my book's lack of market impact was affected by racism. A Chicago television station declined the publisher's request to have me on a midday program by saying, "This would only stir up trouble among the blacks." However, the book's title, while an accurate take on the attitude of those times, was inappropriate. Buyers, not seeing the book displayed, were embarrassed to ask a clerk for the title *They Was Just Niggers.*

Brasch's financial problems ended with bankruptcy four months following publication. Another distributor picked up the book, and I later learned that it sold about 3,000 copies. Yet I only received a partial royalty payment of $260.

But that wasn't the end of the story. An elderly farmer near Moose Lake, Minnesota, called me out of the blue one day and said he'd heard about my Duluth lynching book. (He didn't say he'd read it.) He told me he had lived his entire life on the farm begun by his grandfather more than one hundred years ago. Things had happened on that farm, he said, "that would just boggle you." He said he was offering me a chance to come up to Moose Lake and stay with him for a couple weeks and together we could write the story of his life. "I know the book would be a big deal. I just know it," he emphasized. He said he'd be happy to split the proceeds with me on a fifty-fifty arrangement. He could not afford to pay me anything up front, but knew it would be worth my while to visit him and he'd have stories that would make my head swim. When I asked for an example or two, he said it would be better to talk face to face.

I declined, and to this day wonder why he chose to call me to co-write his autobiography after having heard of my book, which had nothing to do with biography.

Since then I have indeed had offers to ghostwrite autobiographies, but only one was willing to pay for the service. The fellow had spent many years with the federal Bureau of Alcohol, Tobacco, and Firearms (ATF), and recounted numerous richly detailed anecdotes. However, his material only filled about one hundred pages, and I told him we needed almost twice that before a publisher would be interested.

Maybe that was all he had, and I'm not aware his book ever made it into print in those long-ago days before the Internet and print-on-demand e-books that sell for as little as ninety-nine cents.

CHAPTER 9

THREE INCARNATIONS
OF A BOOK

T HE DULUTH LYNCHING STORY RECEIVED A SECOND LIFE IN 1993 when the Off-Broadway producer and book publisher, Harlin Quist, phoned. Quist had left the theater to open an office in Paris where he published numerous luminaries including Eugene Ionesco, Robert Graves, Mark Van Doren, and Edward Gorey, in addition to ascending artists who lavishly illustrated his line of children's books. A few months earlier Quist arrived in Duluth, his hometown, to nurse his ailing mother. He put his Paris and New York operations on hold while tending the elderly woman. But he was bored and looking for something more to do. He envisioned turning the old downtown Norshor movie theater into a center for artists to display their works, for poets to have open mic nights, and for experimental theater to have a home in which to stage new works. He wanted to reissue the lynching book to help underwrite costs of the Norshor enterprise.

Nobody else was offering to republish my book, and what was good enough for Ionesco and Graves was certainly good enough for me. "Let's do it," I told him, and he did.

He retitled the book *Trial By Mob,* and released a nicely designed product. Quist hosted a lavish book release party at the theater that included a production of "Lady Day at Emerson's Bar and Grill." I signed more than sixty books, and though Quist didn't pay an advance, I thought with his promotion moxie *Trial By Mob* would have a decent run.

Five months later I was called by a man from Versa Press, the Illinois company that printed the book, asking if I knew Quist's whereabouts. Quist hadn't paid Versa, his phone had been disconnected, and mail returned with no forwarding address. Did I know anything about this?

I didn't, and never saw Quist again. Several years later, however, his extensive obituary, photo included, appeared in *The New York Times*.

The book which I originally thought might have some traction had endured two failed incarnations, and at that time I estimated my financial remuneration from the book equaled a wage of less than forty cents an hour.

But in the fall of 2000, Sally Rubenstein, an editor at the Minnesota Historical Society Press, called and said the press would like to reissue my book under its Borealis imprint, with the prosaic title *The Lynchings in Duluth*. There'd been a regime change at the Historical Society since the mid-1970s, and now the press believed the book worthy of its sanction.

Because it was a reprint, she could only offer a $500 advance. But hey, it was found money; I didn't have to do anything except sign a new contract with a press that eschewed mention of the book back in 1979. Times and regimes had changed at the Historical Society, and they were eager to take it on. It has had three printings since 2000, and sold more than 12,000 copies under the press's Borealis imprint. The story finally got wide media exposure, from NPR's "All Things Considered," to the "PBS NewsHour" with Jim Lehrer, to a several paragraph mention in Paris's *Le Monde* newspaper. There were also stories in British newspapers, and each year since the 2000 publication I've given four to ten presentations on the topic in school and college classrooms, seminars on race, as well as at Kiwanis, Rotary, and Lions club luncheons.

The city of Duluth has erected an impressive memorial to the victims across the street from where they were hanged in ignominy on that tragic June night in 1920.

May 2017 marked the thirty-eighth anniversary of the initial publication of *The Lynchings in Duluth*. It wasn't a big deal anniversary, but I remembered a discussion with a young entertainment attorney at the original Improv

Comedy Club in Hollywood. Walter Brasch recommended the club for a night out and arranged for me to meet the attorney who represented several independent film producers. The book would be released several months later.

I joined this twenty-something attorney at a table where, between chortles at one-liners delivered by wannabe comics, he said the likelihood of getting an option on the book was remote. "Every author thinks his book would make a great movie," he said. He reported that few studios were actually interested in real books anyway, preferring to see a brief précis or treatment suggesting how the book would work as a film. I thought I could do that, but he told me it would need to be developed by an agent-represented screenwriter before studios would read it. For the moment, I abandoned thinking about a film adaptation for my book.

But the day after a strong review appeared in the *Los Angeles Times*, my phone rang—twice. Both callers identified themselves as agents and asked if studios had contacted me. When I said no, they became animated, saying they'd be in touch as soon as they'd read the book.

Neither called back, and when the book was remaindered less than two years later, I assumed that was the end of the story. However, a friend from Florida Public Television showed the book to a screenwriter with dozens of film credits. He related that the story wasn't sweeping enough for a major studio release, but might work as a made-for-television project. He wasn't optimistic though, because there were no female protagonists in the book, and TV films rely on them for their target audience. Again, I thought end of story.

Then in 1992 when Harlin Quist phoned with his publication offer, he said he'd send the book to some film producers he knew.

Just weeks following Quist's book release, a vice president of a small Hollywood production company called. His team wanted to develop a treatment from my book.

During our discussion he mentioned the earlier assessment that there were no prominent female characters in the story. "But we can fix that," he said. I was offered a contract but no payment. "As soon as we cut a deal you'll get at least $5,000 up front, plus a percent of the net."

Since nobody else was pursuing the book, I signed the contract and waited to see how a screenwriter would translate my work. Although I'd never before seen a film treatment, theirs turned out to be both flimsy and inaccurate. A female heroine had been fabricated and given a major role as a crusading journalist who tried to intervene and prevent the lynchings. But in 1920, few women wrote for daily newspapers, except as society reporters. That was the last I heard from the vice president, and the option expired without notice.

But I subsequently learned a lesson here. A writer should never agree to a film rights contract for his or her work that calls for a percent of the net profit. The reason? There's no such thing as a net profit for any film. Ever. The writer or agent must insist on a share of the gross profit before everything is zeroed out.

In 2000 the documentary of the Duluth tragedy received its third lease on life when the book was re-released, triggering a return of Hollywood's siren song. None of the inquiries came from moguls, though, but rather from hangers-on and screenwriting wannabes seeking permission to develop treatments of the story. One guy thought he could get a finder's fee for bringing the book to a producer's attention. He was something of an insider, he said, having interned at NBC in Burbank. He didn't say where he'd served his internship; it might have been in the mailroom or as a page.

Recently a woman sent an e-mail inquiry assuring me she could get someone interested in filming the book because, "my best friend is Danny Bonaduce's sister." How the sister of an actor best remembered as the red-haired kid Danny from "The Partridge Family" might influence a network to purchase my book eluded me.

I suppose I should be at least mildly flattered that a number of people believed the story should be transferred to celluloid, especially since we're talking about a book that with three incarnations that has sold about 15,000 copies to date.

Over the years I've also learned that only about five percent of properties optioned by Hollywood ever see the big screen. Nonetheless, the film right to my book was purchased by Dale Botten, whose adaptation captured the

2010 $25,000 Expo Grand Prize from *Creative Screenwriter* magazine, and has piqued interest from independent film makers. It's still an uphill battle, but Dale remains doggedly optimistic that his agents will find a home for his award-winning script.

CHAPTER 10

ABOUT GARRISON KEILLOR

UNTIL 1985 I WAS BUSY WITH FITNESS AND HEALTH ARTICLES for several magazines and became a contributing editor of a local runner's tabloid. I had abandoned string assignments for the *Times* after my queries to special sections of the paper were all turned down.

During those good years, my freelance income averaged more than $100 per week, enabling my wife to remain in her then occupation of choice—a stay-at-home-mom.

But 1985 was a turning point. *Runner's World* was sold to Rodale Press and moved its headquarters from Mountain View, California, to Emmaus, Pennsylvania, and hired new editors, to whom I was an unknown. I didn't want to start from scratch, and submit detailed queries when all I needed to do under the Mountain View regime was make a casual phone call and toss a brief pitch, which was usually accepted.

At almost the same time a local health and fitness tabloid, where I'd been regularly published as a contributing editor, closed shop.

There were also editorial changes at other publications in which I was at least occasionally publishing, and within a few months my contacts disappeared. At this stage in my career, I just did not want to go through the laborious process of becoming re-established with new editors who didn't know me.

During that first year my freelance income dropped from nearly $6,000 to $761. The next year, it plummeted even lower: $394, as my slump continued.

I tried writing fiction again and managed to produce one story about a cancer survivor who won a five kilometer alumni race at his college, defeating in the process his old undergraduate nemesis who captured all the awards during the college years. *Inside Texas Running* bought the story for $75.

I blamed persistent back pain for not sitting at the typewriter and developing any writing projects for the next year prior to requiring surgery on the fifth lumbar disk. But then I got lucky. Jeanne Hanson, a literary agent, called me. We didn't know each other well, but she had been in the public relations department at the University of Minnesota, and I'd occasionally get news releases from her when I covered the area for *The New York Times*. She had left the university and had opened an agency. Recently she had been in New York and met with Thomas Dunne, editor at St. Martin's Press, who had a personal imprint with the company, publishing his acquisitions as A Thomas Dunne Book.

Dunne wanted Jeanne to find a Minnesota writer to develop a biography of Garrison Keillor for him. Jeanne offered the gig to one of her clients who ultimately backed away because Keillor said he wouldn't cooperate with the writer, nor would he be interviewed.

Jeanne said she thought the book could be written without Keillor's input and wondered if I were up to the task. She would, of course, represent me should I take the assignment.

I was intrigued; this offer turned 180 degrees the old saw about an author in search of a publisher. I remember thinking even if the final result was mediocre, St. Martin's, being committed, would have to pay half the agreed upon advance—only $8,000, but well beyond anything I'd received for a single project before.

After pondering the offer for no more than a minute, I agreed to take the job.

Jeanne said the proposed title would be *The Man From Lake Wobegon*, and that I should soon expect to hear from Tom Dunne with more particulars.

Actually, Dunne wanted to meet me, so in November Judy and I flew to New York and were treated to an expensive lunch by Dunne before adjourning to a session with him in his office in the Flatiron Building. I don't recall much of our conversation, though I emphasized to him I'd be able to come up with a manuscript despite Keillor's objections.

Upon signing the contract with St. Martin's, I wrote to Keillor informing him of my intention to fulfill the contract, and also expressing an interest in meeting him.

In a handwritten letter he said he was sorry I'd taken the assignment, and that he would in no way cooperate with me, and would request that his friends also decline interviews for the book, which he regarded as an invasion of his privacy. This argument was specious, because Keillor was a public figure, a celebrity, and thus denied the same measure of privacy as non-public persons. In any case, I accepted his refusal to participate and moved on. However, he never knew that had he agreed to talk and demanded the final manuscript edit, I would have granted it to him, not realizing that to have done so would have enabled him to squelch publication of *The Man From Lake Wobegon*. If there's a lesson for novice writers, it is that you never let a subject see or edit your manuscript, unless you are ghost writing it, or co-writing the book with the subject. Some celebrity subjects of ghostwritten biographies who don't bother to look at galleys prior to publication may become like the former pro basketball player, Charles Barkley, who claimed he'd been misquoted in his autobiography.

But Keillor was not passive about his objection to having the book written. He had his attorneys send me a letter indicating the book would be an invasion of Mr. Keillor's privacy, and that I was forbidden to quote from any of his writings should I follow through with the project.

He also contacted people who had been on "A Prairie Home Companion," urging them not to speak to me, and he sent a letter to the superintendent of Independent School District 11, where he had graduated from Anoka High School, indicating that I may be seeking to interview teachers in the district who had taught Keillor. Keillor affirmed that this biography was unauthorized and he hoped his former teachers would not cooperate with me. The superintendent distributed the letter to all of the district's employees.

Retired teachers, however, did not get the missive, and I was able to interview them, as well as disgruntled musicians and other former Minnesota Public Radio employees who were occasionally disparaging of the shy kid from Anoka who'd become this national figure.

I got lucky with Studs Terkel, however, who didn't learn of Keillor's opposition to the book until much later. I called WFMT, the Chicago station where he operated, expecting to get a secretary or answering machine. I was surprised when Studs answered his phone and instantly put me at ease. No appointment was necessary, he said. How much time did I think I needed? I didn't know, but said, "A few minutes." He gave me about twenty and seemed in no hurry to move on. I was then, and remain today, grateful for his generosity in talking about a man he clearly adored, though I assume that generosity wouldn't have been extended had he known Garrison fiercely objected to the bio.

So I was making progress, but it wasn't long after I'd signed the contract, and the proposed bio was mentioned in *People* magazine and the *Los Angeles Times*, that Keillor suddenly announced his departure from his popular radio program, married a former high school classmate, an exchange student from Denmark, and took off for a sabbatical in Copenhagen, away from the prying eyes and ears of American media.

Tom Dunne needed to get the book out before readers completely forgot about Keillor, and I had to both finish researching and writing the book within seven months.

I did it while continuing my full-time teaching at North Hennepin Community College. But the finished product reflects the haste in which it was put together. I missed typos in the galleys, for instance, and regretted not having time to locate other persons who might have shed light on Keillor and his program. But I felt the bio was done as well as possible under trying circumstances. On balance, I thought it was fair, though it leaned more anti than pro Keillor, because the interviews reflected more opinions of folks who didn't think the subject walked on water, than those who revered him. This resulted because Keillor urged those who would have highly regarded him to avoid the interloping biographer.

Following Keillor's resignation, I penned an op-ed article for the old *Los Angeles Herald-Examiner*, stating that I thought the Denmark hiatus would be temporary; Keillor would miss the attention and likely return to his program, which he did about a year later, after *The Man From Lake Wobegon* came out and the notoriety subsided.

Because of Keillor's celebrity, there was buzz that the book might sell as many as 100,000 copies. I allowed myself to think it possible, and that perhaps I could quit my day job and rely on writing to sustain the family's middle-class circumstances.

I was given an insight into what might happen should I try freelancing full-time, however, when I interviewed Wisconsin writer Michael Schumacher. He was doing just that. Schumacher had written a profile on Keillor for *Writer's Digest*, and I was seeking permission to quote from that article. During our conversation, Schumacher talked about his efforts to sustain a reasonable lifestyle as a full-time writer. I recall him saying he refused almost no assignments, including creating advertising copy for matchbook covers, and filing book reviews for several regional weekly newspapers for five or ten dollars a pop, in addition to attempting to secure assignments from magazines that paid well. When desperate for cash, he'd take temporary employment degreasing pits at a nearby American Auto plant. He also pointed out concomitant instability even though he was earning about $30,000 annually. A full-time freelancer might get $16,000 in July, for example, and only $75 in August. Michael said he'd pay off credit cards and the significant accrued interest when flush, and endured home foreclosure threats several times when his bank account hit bottom.

Talking with Michael helped convince me I likely would be unable to cope with wild fluctuations in my financial status, though I did think that as a successful book author, I might count on advances and royalties to keep our family afloat.

At any rate, St. Martin's printed a modest 25,000 copies, and I awaited public reaction.

The *Minneapolis Star Tribune* won a bidding competition with the neighboring *St. Paul Pioneer Press,* paying $1,750 to print a 2,000-word excerpt from the book in its Sunday magazine. But rather than run a chapter, the paper ran snippets and short paragraphs disparately lifted from throughout the text. It did not make for engaging reading.

Once the hardcover book appeared, reviews were mixed between near raves and excoriating detractions chiding me for daring to take on a man revered by millions. And while the book received many reviews, and I made a number of media appearances, the sales staff at St. Martin's was less than enthusiastic about the book. It seems they thought Garrison Keillor was a regional phenomenon then, and stores back east ordered few, if any books. My brother David, a Boston resident, said the book never showed up on the shelves in the Harvard Coop bookstore. And in Minnesota sales were doubly disappointing because after he resigned from the National Public Radio program, Keillor made disparaging remarks about Minnesota that alienated the fan base. They weren't going to buy a book about the formerly beloved author and broadcaster.

Keillor himself called the book dreadfully researched and written.

However, the book did surprisingly well in Nashville, where many musicians were based, and a number of them had performed on "A Prairie Home Companion."

The print run did not sell out, though all remaindered copies quickly disappeared from bookstore bins, and a paperback was issued, for which I received another advance—$2,500.

Several years later, Keillor published a novel *WLT: A Radio Romance*, in which he incorporated a curious epilogue, a sort of *roman à clef*, except most readers wouldn't recognize it, causing some reviewers to wonder what it was all about. The epilogue centered on a community college instructor who was trying to write an unauthorized biography of the novel's main character, a radio celebrity. Before the book was finished, however, the unauthorized biographer was run down by a truck and left brain dead as the novel ended.

Fifteen years after *The Man From Lake Wobegon* came and went, I met one of the former musicians from Keillor's PHC program who said, "We all feared we'd lose the gig if we talked to you. But in the end, most of us got fired anyway." He apologized for not cooperating on the project.

In 1996 during my residency at the Anderson Center for Interdisciplinary Studies in Red Wing, Minnesota, Leif Enger, who would become author of the bestseller *Peace Like a River*, visited the center as a reporter for Minnesota Public Radio. During our brief chat, he suddenly said, "Oh, you're the guy in that epilogue. I always wondered what that was all about, because it didn't seem to fit with the rest of the book."

Regardless, having written this biography did not translate into future book assignments, nor were magazines clamoring for my copy. I've been grateful I didn't quit my day job.

As for Mr. Keillor, in late 2017 he was dumped by Minnesota Public Radio, and *The Washington Post* for inappropriate behavior—bullying, and unwanted sexual advances—toward female employees of his businesses, including the radio programs "Prairie Home Companion," "Writers Almanac" and his St. Paul bookstore. Keillor and many fans believed the MPR response was a vast over-reach. But in follow-up detailed reporting by Laura Yuen, an MPR employee, neither the company nor Keillor come off favorably. MPR apparently failed to address employee concerns for years, attempting to protect its "cash cow." And Keillor's misdeeds, broadcast in Yuen's thorough report, were later posted on the MPR website.

In the spring of 2018, in an agreement with Minnesota Public Radio, his programs were returned to the MPR archives, and he received a settlement of $275,000. Both parties signed off on future litigation. Yet accusations by former employees of "Prairie Home Companion" paint an unflattering portrait of Keillor that may impact sales of a short novel he said he was developing that would reveal his side of this unhappy story, unless terms of the settlement with MPR militate against publication. Assuming the current climate where politicians and celebrities face public exposure for inappropriate behavior toward women, one wonders about reactions from critics and readers, if indeed a publisher releases that manuscript.

CHAPTER 11

CLORIS LEACHMAN AND MAJOR LEAGUERS

THOUGH I WAS DISCOURAGED BY THE SALES OF THE KEILLOR biography, it changed the course of my writing career. Heretofore I had been hesitant to exert my writer's voice, being intimidated, even paralyzed by thinking I had any right to inject opinions into a piece of writing. Reportage was fine; I was comfortable with that, but personal comments were troublesome. After all, I often wondered, who cares what I think? I'm neither sage nor pundit.

But once the contract was signed, I understood that St. Martin's Press wanted this book, and for it to be rejected I'd have to really mess up. That thought was freeing, and I began to assert my voice in that book, and have done so in most of my projects since 1987, when the biography was published.

I took a sabbatical from teaching during the 1988-89 academic year, having earned enough in royalties to make up for income formerly derived from teaching, and as I was contemplating new writing endeavors, a woman from a local public relations firm called pitching an idea.

"You may have read that Cloris Leachman is in town rehearsing for her role as Grandma Moses for the play *Grandma Moses: An American Primitive*, which will be going on tour after it opens here. We're wondering if you'd like to write about that for *The New York Times*."

I said it might be interesting, but I was no longer affiliated with the *Times*.

"Well, we'll be taking the play to Detroit and Phoenix and Portland, and a few other places before it gets to New York. What about newspapers there? We'd give you unlimited access to Cloris and the director, and you could follow the production through its rehearsals, and I bet you'd come up with some pretty good stories."

I was interested. Cloris Leachman was one of the select group of actors who had won both Emmy (she won eight for Primetime, and one for Daytime) and Academy Awards. Beyond that she'd been associated with my old chum Lorenzo Music who had written for the Mary Tyler Moore Show when Cloris was in the cast.

The cast was rehearsing in a St. Paul studio, and I walked in. The director called a break, and I was introduced to Cloris. I was surprised by her height. She couldn't have been more than five-feet or five-one at best. She'd seemed taller on movie and television screens. We spoke briefly, but she was attempting to become the eighty-five-year-old painter during the second act. "I really don't have time now, but why don't you join us tonight for dinner?" She named a then-popular but now defunct restaurant Chez Bananas, in the Minneapolis warehouse district, which had become a favorite of hers.

I brought my very excited and awed wife with me. Cloris was seated at a table with Stephen Pouliot, the playwright, and upon spying me she stood and waved Judith and me to the table.

Conversation, of course, was on the play and her role as Grandma Moses, but it wandered afield to my writing and teaching, about both of which she seemed genuinely interested.

We continued to informally chat at other rehearsals, and I was struck by her humility. No *prima donna*, she dutifully took directions from a local but professional stage director, though his place in the theater pantheon was well below hers. She would politely ask him about motivation for a particular scene and didn't insert herself as a "star" at any time during my presence.

I developed articles for several newspapers, including *The Arizona Republic, Portland Oregonian,* and *Hartford Courant,* profiling Cloris and her Grandma Moses portrayal.

Though she received stellar reviews, the play didn't, and it folded before completing its tour. Ms. Leachman, however, stays active in show biz, and a decade ago at age eighty-two, she was the oldest performer to appear on television's *Dancing with the Stars.*

I had a professional baseball tryout with the Chicago White Sox back in 1957, and had been a lifelong fan as well as avid reader of baseball books. As I began my sabbatical, I thought of trying to write a baseball book, but having done no sports writing since that high school football coverage for the *Superior Evening Telegram,* I had little credibility in pitching a baseball book concept to publishers.

Books on baseball have sold relatively well and had a sort of literary cache because baseball is a thinking-person's game. The other big team sports are athletic and instinctual. Michael Jordan, for instance, couldn't plan specific moves and strategies before or even during the game. Jordan wouldn't say, "When the defender comes close to me, I'll feint left and reverse dribble, if the defender's fooled, be open for a fifteen-foot jump shot." He'd just do it on athleticism and instinct.

A baseball pitcher, however, appraises the batter, decides to start him off with a slow change-up or a slider. The batter is thinking he'll try to put a fast ball on the outside corner of the plate. The manager is pondering whether he should have the runner on first base attempt to steal second on the first or second pitch. And so on.

This quality of the game appeals to literary types and enhances stories told by players.

What kind of stories could I write that hadn't been done before? I might stand a chance with a topic heretofore unexplored.

As a kid I had a copy of *The Encyclopedia of Baseball,* by Hy Turkin and S. C. Thompson. This wondrous tome contained data and statistics on every player who ever performed in a single major league baseball game.

While pondering the literary connection to baseball and how I might contribute to the literature of the game, I had an epiphany. In the long history of the game, there have been one-year wonders whose performances were elevated to stardom or near stardom only once in a career spanning at least five seasons.

During my sabbatical, I spent three days in the library at the National Baseball Hall of Fame in Cooperstown, New York, poring over records and other documents looking for players who fit my criteria. How could a player attain excellence in one season and fail to ever reach such heights again? I ruled out players who'd been outstanding but whose careers were curtailed due to injuries. I looked for players who had not been sidelined by broken limbs, severe sprains, or surgeries, which would have impacted their effectiveness.

Finally, I identified seventeen former big leaguers who enjoyed one season of success amid several that were ordinary to mediocre. With data on their major league tenures, I returned home and wrote letters to all of them, outlining my intention to write about their "one shining season," which became the title of the book.

Though self-addressed stamped envelopes were enclosed for replies, I was somewhat surprised, when after six weeks only one former player, St. Louis Browns pitcher Ned Garver, responded, indicating his willingness to be interviewed. In 1950 Garver won twenty games for his last-place team that won only fifty-four games while losing one hundred that year. A week later I received a second response. This player said he'd be interviewed for $1,000.

I was about to abandon the project, but one evening the phone rang, and the caller identified himself as Joe Black, the 1952 National League Rookie of the Year with the Brooklyn Dodgers. In his first big league season Black had been an outstanding relief pitcher, winning fifteen games for Brooklyn, and saving fifteen others. That year he also became the first African American pitcher to start a World Series game.

Black lasted six years in the major leagues, winning thirty games, before finishing with the Washington Senators at age thirty-three.

Naturally I was interested in his phenomenal rookie season and was surprised that he had phoned. "How many guys said they'd participate?" Black asked.

"One," I said.

"Have any idea why?"

"No."

He began talking about long retired players of his generation who had been grandfathered out of the more generous pension plans that the current players' union had secured from team owners. These were players who may never have earned more than six to ten thousand dollars a year during their careers, and they were bitter at being excluded from the new pension benefits. "These fellows made the game what it is for the guys playing today," Black said. "Many of them will no longer sign baseball cards for free anymore either."

He paused. "Listen, you want to get guys to talk to you, cut 'em a check."

I thanked Black and spent a couple days thinking about what he'd said. Finally, I wrote to the same players again, offering $100 per interview, plus a percent of royalties after the book went to a second printing. This time ten more agreed to participate.

I developed a proposal and on my own dime visited three ex-players and recorded their stories. I drafted a proposal and included chapters on the three interviewees. What I thought was a unique book idea didn't initially fare well with publishers. It received thirty-plus rejections, mostly of the form variety, but among the dozen or so that drew reactions from Jeanne's submissions, half commented that I'd had a solid idea but hadn't executed it very well. The others said the idea was weak, but very well-written, and they'd be pleased to review any other manuscripts from me.

While sometimes editorial comments may be useful, in this case they were only confounding: good idea not well-executed, and well-written, but not compelling stories. There were times I'd wished Jeanne had never shown me those rejections. I hated to abandon the work, however, so began approaching smaller, lesser-known publishers with the manuscript.

Then in one week there were three offers to publish. Jeanne selected the largest operation of the three, Pharos Books, and its modest $5,000 advance. I spent about half of it on the players and travel expenses, personally meeting with each of the eleven.

Curiously, Joe Black wasn't among them. After his baseball career, he'd become an executive with Greyhound Bus in Phoenix. I was headed there to meet with the former Philadelphia Phillies catcher, Stan Lopata, to discuss his glowing statistics of 1956. I assumed I could meet Black in Phoenix as well. But after that phone conversation, he never responded to any of my calls or letters. And even though he was responsible for my project moving forward, in the end he was not a participant himself.

The process of locating and visiting old-time ballplayers was for me both fun and informative. Elderly, retired baseball players are rich story sources, and many, if not most of them, may have only been heard by families and close friends. I was providing opportunities for them to share those stories with a wider audience, plus giving them the chance to reminisce about their big league careers with someone interested enough to record them for a book.

The oldest player in the book was Roger Wolff, a knuckleball pitcher who won twenty games for the 1944 Washington Senators. Wolff lasted seven seasons in the majors, winning only thirty more games in his major league career. He had not been interviewed in nearly forty years before I visited him in his modest home in Chester, Illinois, on an early spring morning in 1989.

A childless widower, Wolff seemed reluctant to have me leave when the interview was completed. He offered to make his favorite bean soup if I stayed for lunch. But another interview waited in a Chicago suburb later that day and I had to depart. Wolff stood in the doorway of his home as I went to my car. "Drive real careful now," he said, in the manner of a grandfather bidding a grandson goodbye.

While there was a sweetness about Mr. Wolff, the most engaging subject was the former Los Angeles Dodgers first baseman, Wes Parker. Parker had always been an excellent fielder, but only an average batter until 1970, when he hit over .300 and drove in more than one hundred runs—both numbers far above any other of his nine major league seasons.

Parker was an anomaly among professional athletes; born to a wealthy family, well-educated and cultured, Parker and I briefly discussed the childhood compositions of Wolfgang Amadeus Mozart. Parker had also worked as an actor and TV sports analyst post baseball. Most important, however, was that he could precisely explain why he'd had that magnificent season in 1970.

"I decided to show everybody that I could be a good hitter in the big leagues," he said. "I made sacrifices to do that like giving up an active social life and sleeping ten hours a night. I concentrated on nothing but baseball that year and proved I could succeed. But you know what? At the end of the season, I decided it wasn't worth that hermit existence. That wasn't me. There was more to life than just baseball, and I wanted to take advantage of that."

William Faulkner's adage about doing away with grandma if it enhanced a writer's chances for publication could also apply to an athlete who might do anything to be an all-star performer. Except, of course, for the grounded and well-rounded Wes Parker.

Hana Umlauf Lane, my editor at Pharos Books, secured Ira Berkow, the noted sports columnist at *The New York Times* to write the introduction, and probably for that reason, it was favorably reviewed in the Sunday *Times Book Review*.

Kirkus, a book review publication for libraries, said it was "One of the more curious baseball books of this or any season." A reviewer at the *Ottawa Citizen* in Canada said the book was "brilliantly written," and Bill Littlefield, author and host of National Public Radio's "Only a Game," praised it on his program.

But again, the first print run didn't sell out, and I earned nothing beyond my advance.

A factor may have been that United Media, which had established Pharos Books primarily as the book publishing enterprise for cartoon collections by "Peanuts" creator Charles Schultz, and for *The World Almanac*, was sold within a year after issuing *One Shining Season*. The new owner merged Pharos's backlist, but reportedly purchased that press to get rights to the Almanac. *One Shining Season*, however, did not fade to ignominy; it retains a life at Amazon.com and eBay, and is in fact listed in a 2013 volume by Ron Kaplan, *501 Baseball Books Fans Must Read Before They Die.*

CHAPTER 12

WITH DONALD McCAIG IN HIGHLAND COUNTY

THE YEAR BEFORE TAKING EARLY RETIREMENT FROM TEACHING, I spent a week at a sheep farm run by the author and National Public Radio "All Things Considered" essayist, Donald McCaig. I'd seen a small advertisement in the magazine *Poets & Writers*, offering a writer's cottage at his Williamsville, Virginia (population 16) farm for $100 per week.

Though not particularly drawn to bucolic settings—with or without sheep—the price was right and I needed a respite from teaching and a chance to recover from my disappointment over failure to interest a publisher in my short story collection.

At that time I knew Donald McCaig as a contributor to NPR's "All Things Considered," but had not yet read any of his books. (Several years following our visit, McCaig was tapped by the Margaret Mitchell estate to write *Rhett Butler's People*, a *Gone with the Wind* sequel, with a million-copy press run.) I learned that in 1971 he had abandoned a lucrative career as an advertising mogul in New York for a dilapidated farmhouse that he and his wife, Anne, restored. There they had set about raising sheep and training border collies. I was intrigued by a man who, unlike many 60s-era back-to-the-land proponents, remained committed to the ideals of the counterculture.

Prior to our arrival, McCaig told us not to expect resort amenities. The place, though adequate, was Spartan, he wrote. "It's quiet here and if you get down to it, you can get quite a bit (of writing) done."

Tiny Williamsville seemed frozen in the 1930s. While we saw no goat carts or horse-drawn wagons, rusted autos rested in farmyards, presumably to be cannibalized for the useable vehicle du jour. Dotted with marginal farms, the region's buildings and hollow-eyed inhabitants called to mind Depression-era photographs by Walker Evans and Dorothea Lange. "Any farmer here in Highland County, making $10,000 a year is doing relatively well," McCaig told me.

The rental cottage, a short hike from the Cowpasture River, at the foot of geode-spawning Bullpasture Mountain, had been erected in a pasture full of thistles and tall grass that hid mounds of sheep spoor we had to negotiate on our way to the tiny two-hole outhouse fifteen paces from the front door. Masking tape crisscrossed one hole, and affixed above it was a hand-lettered "Out of order" sign that probably reflected McCaig's puckish humor.

The cottage was an austere one-room affair with strips of flypaper dangling from the rafters. Aside from the drone of bugs and the gurgling of the nearby river, it was quiet at the farm. We woke each morning to the bleating of sheep and McCaig's whistling as he coaxed his dogs through herding routines. During the first three days at the cottage, I felt blocked, despite McCaig's sense that the serenity could elicit production. Apparently I needed to adjust to an absence of ambient suburban sounds—lawnmowers, cars, or children at play. Finally I began an essay I would complete upon returning home.

Near the end of the week, I exchanged books with McCaig. He gave me his memoir, *An American Homeplace*, and I gave him *One Shining Season*. He had declined my offer of *The Man From Lake Wobegon*, which I had published eight years earlier. "I don't care to read about Garrison Keillor," he told me. "We cover the same sort of territory, and I don't need to know anything more about him. But baseball's another matter."

During my stay, McCaig offered writerly advice. "Believe in your work," he said. "Stay the course. But don't teach writing if you don't have to. Your students assume you will mentor them forever, and you could spend weeks every year reading their probably unpublishable manuscripts, and struggle to find graceful ways to tell them that. No matter what you say, and how you say it, they'll be hurt and angry. In my experience, you'll avoid this unpleasantness by declining teaching gigs from the get-go."

This was advice to which I did not hearken, and of course, McCaig was right. Years after I stopped teaching creative writing, I continue to receive correspondence from former students requesting reactions to books and other pieces they have written, along with anticipation that I will recommend an agent or a publisher for the manuscript.

However, I continue that practice anyway. I recall the kindness of Richard Armour, and several editors who, while rejecting my work, took time to offer encouragement and hope. Writers may be blessed with talent, but getting published is a struggle all along the way for most. A few encouraging words from a practitioner who has been through the process can often help the fledgling writer to continue.

Following my early retirement, a severance package enabled me to begin writing full-time, free of financial stresses. A year or so prior to exiting education, I'd returned to my first love, creating short stories.

I had recently managed to complete a story begun several years before. Its genesis was a Canadian fishing trip back in 1994, and it had stalled. One day, I revisited the story and the conclusion which had long vexed me. Now, the ending was obvious. How could I have missed it all those years? I quickly finished the piece, sending it to the tony outdoor magazine, *Gray's Sporting Journal*. They bought it for a nice fee, and Mike Derr (naturally) reprinted "That Wildwood Summer." It was the only short story I'd written in years that wasn't humor or satire, as would be all of the stories that followed.

The next several years were the most productive of my writing life. Free from the attention of the day job, I was on a roll, turning out story after story, almost effortlessly, it seemed, and placing each one with relative ease. One of them stemmed from an off-handed remark by Judy after she'd purchased a new guitar and said she'd like to play the blues. As noted earlier, I noodled with that notion and came up with the story "The Ladies of West Rarington Falls Get Down."

The story received some attention; a literary agent called to see if I had a novel in the works, and the story was posted online, where it remained for more than five years. However, the story was not well received by some women.

I read the story to those assembled at Arts Workshop International in Assisi, Italy, and a number of women of the approximate ages of those in the story were upset. My friend and author, Bob Lacy, used the story in his fiction writing classes at The Loft and found similar responses from many women taking his class. I vaguely recall reading a psychologist—perhaps Theodor Reik—as an undergraduate and discovering that women were less likely than men to embrace satire. Women tended more than men to empathize with the satirized. I didn't regard my story as satire, so much as a dialectic: elderly women who belong to garden clubs and symphony societies trying to embrace the blues as experienced by rural southern African Americans.

I took some heat for the blues ladies story, but not nearly as much as resulted from an essay about contemporary classical music that the *Christian Science Monitor* printed a few years back. "Why Does Modern Classical Music Spurn Melody?" went mini-viral.

In that essay I opined that orchestras loose audiences by commissioning new compositions that are void of melody. I argued that many modern pieces are intellectual exercises, but that listeners have, and expect, emotional connections with music, classical or otherwise.

The piece appeared on numerous websites, including public radio stations and major symphony orchestras. Many visitors to these sites posted comments, and I include a representative sample here, roughly proportional to the pros and cons.

This is definitely one of the most irresponsible of the New Music hatchet jobs I've seen.

This is smug personal taste masquerading as criticism, and for any commenter who is compelled to reach for political arguments, Mr. Fredo (sic) is telling everyone how music should be, and how it should be more something that pleases him, while at the same time not even bothering to listen to contemporary classical music that is full of melody.

Music critics, and arts critics in general, seem not to be rooted in the audiences for which they write. They are very much like a certain part of the political spectrum who insist that they know what is good for you, in spite of what you might like or what your common sense tells you. I might suggest an impolite walk out during the next "Concerto for Two Buses and Orchestra." The critics might notice, and the conductors who select these things certainly will.

The article is childish in that it shows the writer to be publishing material that he clearly knows very little about. That alone is offensive, let alone the actual content of the writing.

Thank God, somebody sounds off in this direction. I have grown up and have been imbued with classical music and play it to the total exclusion of this so-called "modern" cacophony.

In the Internet age, when writing for publication, one must be prepared to become unpopular in some circles. On the other hand, there's the cliché that it is better to get a negative notice than no notice at all. And regarding my essay, at least it provoked controversy, and the discussion continues.

CHAPTER 13

GOOD EDITORS
(They Liked My Stuff)

UPON COMPLETING *ONE SHINING SEASON,* I BEGAN ASSEMBLING A batch of previously published reminiscences situated in the mostly Scandinavian neighborhood in Duluth where I was raised. Many of these featured my great aunt, Hilma Norquist, who lived next door with her sister-in-law (my maternal grandmother), and Mother's unmarried sister, Ada.

Many of these stories, all set during my boyhood, were published in *Lake Superior Magazine,* and readers seemed to enjoy Hilma's quiddities, as well as the situations in which she often found herself during the course of daily life.

Besides *Lake Superior Magazine,* other pieces had appeared in *Minnesota Monthly,* the old *Los Angeles Herald-Examiner,* and the *St. Paul Pioneer Press.* I gathered sixteen of these stories and gave them the title *Chronicles of Aunt Hilma, and Other East Hillside Swedes.* Of those sixteen, fourteen were decidedly humorous, thanks to my great aunt and uncle Howard. The other two were more poignant sketches, but they nicely melded into the flow of the rest. I sold the book to North Star Press of St. Cloud, a regional operation, and it followed on the heels of *One Shining Season,* giving me two books published for 1991.

There was no advance for the Hilma stories, and I don't think it earned much more than a thousand dollars in royalties. I wasn't terribly disappointed, because I'd already been paid for the individual pieces and that thousand necessitated minimal extra effort.

I believe sales were hindered somewhat by a negative review in the *Duluth News Tribune* that centered on one of the clearly unfunny stories. It was about an adult man who attended Saturday morning serials during the late 1940s at downtown movie theaters. The man, mentally handicapped, wore cowboy duds to the theater and fired his cap pistols at the screen during western films. So did a lot of other kids. Angelo, however, was probably in his thirties, and was occasionally teased by some of the older kids. The reviewer pointedly said she saw nothing funny about abusing Angelo. She clearly missed the point; this was not meant to be humorous, and nearly three decades later I still wonder how anyone, let alone a reviewer, assumed I considered this risible material.

A former state senator once told me that in nearly every elected body the great breadth of the population is truly represented—well-educated, marginally-educated, brilliant, mediocre, even astoundingly uninformed. The same thing may well be true of reviewers, regardless of how they perceive your book—or mine.

In early January 1995, I drafted a short story in one sitting, tweaked it over the next several days and sent it off to Robley Wilson, long-time editor of the *North American Review*, the longest continuously published literary journal in the country. Inside the back cover editors used to print a letter from Thomas Jefferson in which he sent payment for a subscription to *NAR*.

My story was titled "Lunch With Jackie Cliff: Oscar Winner," and the story was written to look like a magazine interview with a young man who won Hollywood's first Academy Award given for best boys.

The story was seen by Mike Derr, then editor of *America West Airlines Magazine* who phoned one day and asked to reprint it. He offered $150. NAR paid $50—a decent sum for a small-circulation literary magazine—and Mike would pay triple that amount to reprint it. I of course agreed, and he asked if I had anything else in a similar vein that he might like. It didn't matter if the story appeared elsewhere first, he said.

Thus began a seven-year relationship with Mike, the best magazine editor I've ever worked with. It's easy to say that, I suppose, because Mike loved most of my submissions, which came to include essays as well as short stories. On more than one occasion I had two pieces in the same issue of his in-flight magazine. He also wrote a nice review of my 2003 novel, *Indians in the Arborvitae*, for Amazon. With a few alterations, I had worked a couple of the stories Mike published into that novel.

One of the stories Mike bought was titled "Finito, Inc.," taking its lead from the wag who said, "It ain't over 'till the fat lady sings." In my story, a rotund contralto organized a group of portly ladies who would be hired to sing arias to terminate corporate board meetings, university faculty senate sessions, and similar events. I heard from folks who thought this was a great idea and I might want to copyright "Finito, Inc." so no one could capitalize on my creation. It wouldn't bother me if someone did. I'm bereft of business acumen.

But there was another story written in the manner of a newspaper or magazine feature in which the International Olympic Committee sanctioned quilting as a winter Olympic sport. The American squad was comprised of septuagenarian women who were thrilled to be finally considered athletes and were proud to wear Team USA sweats. I mentioned that one of the team members was taking Quinidine for heartbeat irregularity.

Despite the posting at the top of the story's first page stating, "Fiction by Michael Fedo," some readers assumed it was non-fiction.

I was very surprised one morning to receive a phone call from a man who introduced himself as the director of publications at a large U. S. pharmaceutical firm. He said he'd read my story on his way back from Phoenix and had passed it around to his staff. All of them, he said, thought it was a great "article."

Then came the kicker. "We'd like you to do a follow-up for one of our magazines," he said. "Talk to the women again, and see what other meds they might be taking. You may know that we manufacture Quinidine and Coumadin, and our people would be very interested in such a story. I can pay you $1,000, plus expenses for a 1,500-word article."

A pregnant pause. "Um, sir, that was fiction; it was all made up."

Another pause on his end, then, "Oooh, do I have egg on my face."

One time I departed from Mike Derr, who never paid more than $600 for a story, and sent "The Wedding Reviewer" to *American Way*, a thick, tony slick, à la *The Atlantic* that was published for American Airlines. They paid $1,100 for an accepted story. "The Wedding Reviewer" was about a newspaper reporter who critically reviewed local weddings for the daily in a fictional backwater community before ascending to major metropolitan dailies. I gave fictitious names to each of the newspapers.

I was very pleased to have the story accepted there, but baffled a couple weeks later when I was called by the magazine's fact checker. Several of the towns I mentioned in the story did not appear in any atlases he consulted.

"I took literary license," I said. "They're fictitious."

"Oh," he replied. "Then I suppose the newspapers in those towns you mention are fictitious too."

Several weeks after that first *American Way* publication, I finished another story and mailed it off to them. Again, it was accepted, and scheduled for several months down the road. Unfortunately, I learned from an editor a month later that management had determined to no longer publish fiction. I couldn't keep my check for the story, because the magazine paid contributors following publication. I promptly sent Mike Derr the story, and bless his heart, he took it and featured "Iron Mike in Melda's Garage" on the cover.

The story had a goofy conceit, based on a friend telling me about a teaching colleague whose husband believed he could at age forty-eight become a designated hitter for an American League baseball team, so he bought an Iron Mike pitching machine to practice batting in his garage all winter. The notion highly amused everyone but my friend's colleague who feared her husband was losing his marbles. My friend shook his head relating this information, then said, "That guy had no marbles to lose in the first place."

I used his line in the story about such a man, except my character was in his fifties, and in the process, enjoyed success of a sort because he parlayed his baseball attempt into appearances on Johnny Carson and small roles in Hollywood movies. Later the story became a finalist for a Maggie—awarded by the Western Publishers Association for best fiction appearing in a magazine published west of the Mississippi.

But the fun ended when Mike Derr was sacked. He called me with the news saying that management believed he was trying to turn the magazine into a print version of National Public Radio, or a *New Yorker* knockoff. I.e., he was publishing my stuff, and the sharp and witty essays of my long-time coffee chum, Robert Lacy.

. Neither of us ever had so encouraging an editor as Mike Derr, and we commiserated constantly about his sad departure, and our perhaps sadder loss. That sadness was compounded after we learned Mike died in January 2013 from brain cancer.

CHAPTER 14

THE CHANGING LANDSCAPE

O NE STORY OF MINE—NOMINATED FOR A PUSHCART AWARD, given to the best stories appearing in a calendar year in the nation's small press magazines—was rejected by Mike for reasons I no longer recall. Perhaps it was too esoteric, but it remains one of my favorite stories. Titled "The James Boys, Summer, 1881," it is built around a chance encounter between Frank and Jesse, and William and Henry in Hannibal, Missouri. Henry, residing in England, was visiting brother William, but grew bored. William arranged for a lecture tour that would take them into the American heartland and rejuvenate his novelist brother.

Meanwhile, Frank and Jesse had seen flyers announcing the two celebrated East Coast intellectuals, and thought they might be related, so they went to the visitors' hotel room where they shared whiskey (Jesse, a teetotaler, drank tea), and swapped anecdotes. As the story develops, it seems that suggestions by the outlaws become titles of books by the literary brothers. For example, Frank talks about settling a score with a Union sympathizer farmer named Poynton, burning his buildings and absconding with his animals. "Yessir," he says, "We made off with them spoils of Poynton's." Henry writes this down, and later delivers his novel *The Spoils of Poynton*. It was fun to imagine the scene and write that story, which ran in a now long-defunct literary journal, and later appeared in an online literary magazine (alas, also now extinct), which nominated it for the Pushcart.

This story received nearly two dozen rejections before its initial acceptance. I suppose at my age I've become something of an old scold but I think the reason for the story's circulation from periodical to periodical over nearly three years is that many younger editors are probably not familiar with the literary James brothers, consequently they missed the cues placed throughout the story indicating the possibility that William's and Henry's subsequent works were suggested, albeit inadvertently, by Jesse and Frank, or the town of Hannibal, Missouri, in which I placed a saloon called The Golden Bowl, that became a novel by Henry James. In my story, Henry also uses a quote from Jesse about a "turn of the screw," to title another novel.

Meanwhile Frank James's quotes about "Habit is the flywheel of society..." and "An act has no ethical quality whatever..." were absorbed by William in his later works.

Editors unfamiliar with some of Henry and William's writings would not have caught these references, and I suppose I'm revealing myself as something of a literary snob in that regard, but so be it.

Coinciding with Mike Derr's departure from the inflight magazine, the Internet's influence decimated many print journals to which freelance writers contributed. Some of these magazines simply ceased publication in print and moved online. Those that did this substantially reduced pay for contributions. For instance, I sold an essay to *The World & I* for $500. When they moved to an online journal they paid only $50 for a piece of similar length, and I ceased sending material to the Internet version.

The industry was shaking out, and a lot of freelancers fell from the trees. Bob Lacy and I have not quite adjusted to the new parameters, and have more or less gone kicking and complaining into the new world of publishing realities.

I won't carp about everything the Internet does, including reducing pay for freelancers; indeed, I write for online publications myself, among those that don't pay. These days I mostly write op-ed essays when something gets up my nose, and since op-ed page editors nationwide have had their freelance budgets slashed, I may not even send my pieces to places like the *St. Paul Pioneer Press*, the *Hartford Courant*, *Providence Journal*, *Newsday*, or the *Chicago Tribune*, newspapers where I'd heretofore enjoyed a good reception, placing at least two or three essays in each of those.

So when overcome by the urge to opine about something, I'm usually sending it someplace like *MinnPost*. I like the immediacy of these online publications because almost always there are reader comments posted within an hour or two following its appearance, and I appreciate that. Readers will respond to online postings with far greater frequency than they will editorials that appear in print. Of the hundred or so pieces I've published in newspapers, I can count on both hands the number than have elicited reader responses, pro or con. Whereas when publishing online, I've rarely failed to get at least one response, and several essays have received more than a dozen replies.

For nearly ten years in the 1990s, I taught writing classes in creating op-ed articles, personal essays, and humorous fiction at The Loft Literary Center. Classes, excepting the op-ed courses, were comprised almost entirely of women. Not surprising, since male culture has chosen to be post-literate, and no longer values reading, let alone writing.

But it was the op-ed classes that drew the most student interest, and I continued with it for a few years beyond the others I'd taught. I encountered students who wrote extremely fine pieces that seemed eminently publishable, and indeed, a number of my students published editorials before our sessions ended.

There was one chap though, a fellow in his forties, who was active in critiquing the work of other students, and who often brought his own creations to read to the class. At our third or fourth session, he read a piece that I thought was a decent start, and I encouraged him to consider some student comments as well and see if incorporating a few might improve chances of publication.

"I already sent it out," he said.

We wished him well, and I said it might be wise to hearken to the class comments should the piece be rejected. But the very next day it appeared on the op-ed page of the *Minneapolis Star Tribune*.

What did this mean? Did the class members and I totally miss the mark on that essay? Any editor can be wrong, re old Harry Davis. The other male in the class approached me the next week and said, "I thought Ernie's essay was a first draft and needed more work. But it got published anyway."

"You only have to please one person with your writing," I said. "But that one person is the editor who can buy or reject it. This guy bought. What more can I say?"

I finally abandoned teaching a couple years after Donald McCaig told me to never teach writing. But that had little to do with why I stopped. For some reason the op-ed course drew what seemed to me an inordinate number of left-brained pupils, with proclivities toward structure and numbers. "How long should an essay be?" "How can you tell if a sentence is too long?" "How do you know when to begin a new paragraph?" "How do you know when your editorial is finished?"

I wasn't expecting to offer primers on writing, and I assumed folks took Loft classes because they felt they might be able to write well and had probably earned As and Bs in English classes at school. My responses to these queries dismayed many of my left-brained acolytes. Other faculty were of no help to me because they claimed to have never encountered such students, whereas I seemed to get one or two each term. They were the ones who hung around after class, until after 10 PM, practically insisting I tell them how to make their pieces publishable. They didn't get notions like flow, or transitions, or pacing, demanding I give examples, then not comprehending when I did, or at least try to convey what I meant by telling them the piece wasn't working. Finally, I couldn't help them make it "work," because they seldom understood what made awkward sentences awkward. It became too much for me, and I left teaching for good back in 2002.

CHAPTER 15

THREE MORE
BOOKS

I N 2002 MY ART TEACHER WIFE HAD AGREED TO ACCOMPANY THE
French teacher at the high school where she taught, and a batch of her students, on a two-week tour through France. I was invited to go along too,
and we prepared for the excursion though I didn't think we could make the
trip without taking out a loan. This concern was allayed when the Minnesota
Historical Society Press contacted me with an offer that I might not have accepted, except the $5,000 advance would easily pay for our trip.

Between 1879 and 1885 a man named Warren Upham, a state of
Minnesota geological surveyor, traversed the state on foot and horseback, visiting fifty counties. Upon completion, he began compiling *Minnesota Place
Names*, and included 20,000 entries detailing the naming of counties, cities,
rivers, lakes, and forests. The massive tome was a mainstay in libraries, but far
too cumbersome for travelers in Minnesota to put in automobile glove com-
partments.

More than seventy years after Upham's volume was published, the
Historical Society Press wanted a *Pocket Guide to Minnesota Place Names*, an
abridged version of the Upham opus.

They asked me to do it. My original reluctance—overcome by the $5,000
advance—softened, and I agreed.

My task was to reduce Upham's 20,000 entries to about 1,200 for an easy
to tote paperback volume. The assignment called for inclusion of every county,
every county seat, and each town with a population exceeding 10,000. I was

free to include places with unique names or histories, and I would also update the more archaic expressions and descriptions employed by Warren Upham those long decades ago. Cheekiness was allowed by the editors. There's a village and lake called Buzzle that Upham noted was named for an early settler. I added "That is all we know of Buzzle, and all we need to know." Then there was the Diarrhoea River, named for what was thought to result when its water was consumed. For commercial and recreation purposes, however, in 1911 its name was changed by area residents to the prosaic Greenwood River. I wonder if any canoers on the Greenwood River would swim in it or eat its fish if they knew its original name. Looneyville took its name from an early settler, and that's no joke. Nodine got its name from surveyors who couldn't find an eating establishment in the area. And "Snowball is no more, having been destroyed by fire. Its demise calls to mind the phrase, 'a snowball's chance in hell.'"

Assembling this text turned out to be both fun and informative. I absorbed more state history than I'd ever learned in classes, and years after publication I still get occasional calls from media—radio stations in particular—asking for comments on the development of a particular community, or to expand on the genesis of its unusual name.

In February 2002, I started merging several of my published short stories into a comic novel, to which I added about 15,000 words of new text. This book was titled *Indians in the Arborvitae*, and the title was inadvertently suggested by Glenn Thorpe, my father-in-law.

On the fifty-second wedding anniversary of Glenn and Gloria Thorpe, Judy gifted them with a brace of arborvitae shrubs. Glenn went out of his way to praise the shrubs, but kept asking where they should be placed. He brought up the subject several times during the day, each time Judy suggesting appropriate placement possibilities.

At one point he said, "These are very nice, but you should have them. They'd be better at your place."

Judy protested; she'd bought them as a gift for her parents. But Glenn remained obdurate. "Take them home with you."

Judy asked what was wrong, and Glenn finally spoke. "You know, they grow real high and get sort of bushy. Out in the country here, Indians from the reservation would come and hide behind those bushes and when we'd leave they might come in and steal our stuff."

Glenn was serious, and we had to return home with his arborvitae, albeit enjoying a hearty laugh over his reasoning. "There's gotta be a story in this," I said to Judy.

And, of course, there was. But the manuscript wasn't well received, in large part because it was only about 35,000 words in length. Several publishers noted this, and said if the length could be doubled they'd take another look.

On the one hand I understood this. As the prices of books—particularly hardcover copies—typically run from $25 to $40, it is presumed the book buyer wants some bulk when the book is handled. Publishers assume the customer will feel cheated if the book runs only 150 or so pages. They may be right, but I'm with the late novelist Elmore Leonard who famously said, "I leave out the stuff that readers skip over." So do I, and the story I'd written was the appropriate length. Adding to it would have meant putting in another hundred pages that readers would have skipped or skimmed.

The book was what it was, though I initially attempted to work more pages into the story, but finally kept the book as originally completed and began sending it to small, independent presses.

On the same day two publishers made offers on the book, and I chose Green Bean Press only because it was based in New York. The other offer came from a St. Louis firm, which I thought lacked the cachet of a New York address.

The book came out as a slim paperback and managed to get a few reviews in newspapers and online sites. Because the main characters are an American studies high school teacher and his widowed father, the book seemed especially popular with teachers. This may sound like a broken record, but within a year of publication, Green Bean Press folded, making three of my book publishers and even more magazines to which I contributed victims of financial instability, leaving me to sometimes wonder if or how my work contributed to those failures.

Indians in the Arborvitae, which one reviewer described as "non-stop laughs," while another said I'd written a story about two men—a father and son—searching for love, and though I wasn't aware of that during the writing and editing of the book, her comment whacked me upside the head, and darned if that woman wasn't right. The book hasn't been in stores for years but remains available through Amazon, and I retain a hundred or so copies in a large box in the basement, which could be happily dispensed to interested readers. And unlike Amazon I'll pay for postage and shipping.

What would eventually become my eighth published book was actually the first one I wrote.

This story begins on August 5, 1967, the day Judy and I were married in Spooner, Wisconsin, her hometown. At the reception, my father sat with Judy's maternal grandfather, Henry Wood, and some time later Dad told me that the old fellow had talked about his life as an entertainer. Henry had toured the country during the first third of the century with old-time medicine and tent shows, playing in mostly rural areas. He told Dad about several adventures and misadventures, which amused my father. Since I'd been writing for magazines and newspapers, Dad thought I might find Henry's story interesting.

About eight months later I had a chance to interview Henry, thinking perhaps I might place an article about those turn of the century theatricals into a scholarly article which would enhance my prospects for tenure at Stout. But Henry was an uneducated man, having only completed third grade before beginning his employment with a medicine show, and I assumed this would negate publication in an academic journal.

Still, I managed to get an amusing story about his difficulty in finding a retirement home because a landlord remembered the villainous Henry Wood in those old melodramas of the era, and could not or would not distinguish between Henry off-stage and the characters he portrayed onstage. *The Christian Science Monitor* ran the piece in 1971.

After Henry's wife Bessie died in 1974, however, he began visiting relatives, staying a few days with each before hurrying off.

He spent two days with us, and as I'd recently learned his theatrical memorabilia had been destroyed in a house fire a couple years earlier, I thought to record his stories for a family legacy. We spent an entire day putting his anecdotes on an old reel-to-reel tape recorder, and after he left I transcribed the tapes and following some editing and rearranging, typed up a manuscript, which I gave to Judy's mother on our Fourth of July picnic. She made copies of that typescript for her five sisters, and I assumed that was the end of the story.

But at Thanksgiving 2008, Jackie Theriot, one of Judy's aunts, gave me a bound copy of Henry's story that her son had privately printed for the family.

Thirty-four years after our interview, I re-read Henry's account of that long-ago life and decided this was a story worth telling, worth hearing about, and that would add to the lore of American theater history.

I sent the book to the Wisconsin Historical Society Press because most of the story was rooted in Wisconsin where Henry lived nearly all of his eighty-two years when he wasn't on the road. The editor was quite interested in the project, but it was rejected apparently because Henry's first-person story couldn't be thoroughly fact-checked. At least that's what the editor said.

So I sent it next to the Minnesota Historical Society Press, publishers of *The Lynchings in Duluth* and *The Pocket Guide to Minnesota Place Names*.

They accepted the manuscript and offered a $1,000 advance. Nonprofit presses can't afford large advances, and authors submitting to such publishers should not expect to be paid anywhere near what most commercial publishers can offer. The upside of having a title with a university or historical society press is that the book stays in print far longer than it would with a for-profit company.

I had enjoyed an excellent relationship with this press and happily signed a contract. But in a state legislative wrangle, the budget for the operations at the Historical Society Press suffered draconian slashes; the publishing arm lost editorial positions and was forced to cancel several books that had been accepted, mine included.

It was the second time in my career that a piece of writing had been "de-accepted." The first was a short story that a Florida-based outdoors magazine editor took, but his publisher nixed after reading it in galley proofs. The problem was that the story, "Angling for Highbrows," was a spoof on TV fishing programs, and the owner/publisher sponsored one of those shows.

Several years prior to reconstructing Henry Wood's story and titling it *A Sawdust Heart: My Vaudeville Life in Medicine and Tent Shows*, I had been asked by Todd Orjala, then an acquisition editor at the University of Minnesota Press, to read a proposal for a book about mob violence in Minnesota. I gave a thumbs up to the proposal, which the press released under the title *Legacy of Violence: Lynch Mobs and Executions in Minnesota*, by John D. Bessler, husband of a future senator, Amy Klobuchar.

I thought perhaps as a favor to me Todd might be willing to read my manuscript. Before I sent him the manuscript, however, I determined to augment Henry's story by seeing if there were any printed traces of his show business career. He'd said that he toured with the Brooks Stock Company, among several others, and fortunately Maude Brooks, matriarch of the company, had left her memorabilia with the Jackson County Historical Society in Maquoketa, Iowa. There Judy and I uncovered a couple photos of Henry on stage and off, along with historical accounts of where the Brooks company toured. I also learned of The Theatre Museum of Repertoire Americana in nearby Mt. Pleasant, and was able to glean several valuable anecdotes and pages for the manuscript before sending it to Todd. Two months later Todd said the University of Minnesota Press would be proud to publish *A Sawdust Heart*. He also offered a $2,000 advance against royalties, and since its 2011 publication, the book has found a niche audience among old troupers and theatre historians.

CHAPTER 16

A LOOK AT NONPROFIT PUBLISHERS

THOUGH THE ADVANCE FROM *A SAWDUST HEART* HAS NOT YET been recovered, I've augmented the book's income through speaking engagements to historical societies in towns where Henry's portrayals of villains had been performed, as well as at the Mt. Pleasant museum, and in southern Wisconsin, where Henry lived.

Meanwhile, over the nearly five decades I've been publishing my work, there numbered nearly one hundred essays and profiles, many of which seemed not dated, and of possible reader interest. I picked three dozen of them and in late 2012 sent them off to Todd Orjala for his assessment.

The University of Minnesota Press, like most nonprofit publishers, does not have a bevy of interns and entry-level assistant editors as first readers who screen manuscripts for their supervisors. Consequently, manuscripts pile up on an acquisition editor's desk, or are backlogged on his or her computer. In short, potential authors must anticipate a longer than normal wait before learning they've been rejected or accepted.

Many university publishers will send out manuscripts for peer review—especially when there's an academic component to the proposed book. This would be especially true should the subject be biography, history, or science.

The problem for authors under these circumstances is that the review process may take two years or longer because the reviewers—usually professors—are only offered a small honorarium to complete the task, and are likely to put the review on low priority.

Several years ago, after a friend labored nearly ten years on a literary biography, he submitted it to a Midwestern university press. The editor praised the manuscript and wanted to send it out for three reviews. He asked for and received an exclusive consideration during this process. When my friend informed me after the fact that he agreed to the exclusive, I groaned, then cautioned him that he should not in the future grant any press a review process like that which could tie up his manuscript for months or longer.

More than twenty-two months later his manuscript was rejected, and he was so depressed that it took him almost two years before he made another submission. This story, however, has a happy ending; the book was published and nominated for awards in biography.

The twenty-two-month wait was, I believe, unconscionable, and if an author eager for publication should be faced with similar demands for exclusive consideration, he or she should feel free to stipulate a specific period under which the manuscript remains out of circulation. I'd put this at no longer than six to eight months.

Todd had my manuscript several months, and I hadn't heard from him, so I sent a brief inquiry regarding the status of the manuscript. He said he liked much of it but wanted more time, which I granted. Nearly a year after the submission, we met for lunch, at which time he reiterated that he liked the essays, but wanted them to be somewhat linked. "Our books about Duluth have done quite well for the press," he said. "In this collection you probably have twenty or so that are at least tenuously connected to Duluth. Think about adding another eight or ten and I think we'll have something."

I went home and the magic of my early post-retirement years returned; I finished a dozen essays within six weeks, and even managed to place several for magazine publication. Not a big thing, except there were several hundred dollars for payment; without Todd's prodding, I'd not have even considered writing those essays.

Before Todd left the University of Minnesota Press, we had titled the work *Zenith City: Stories from Duluth*. My working title was *A Zenith City Memoir*, but Todd and other editors at the press determined that almost no one outside of Duluth would recognize its "Zenith City" sobriquet, and that title would limit the book's appeal.

While my hometown people and places have clearly influenced my work, in many of the pieces, Duluth could just as easily be replaced with Concord, Des Moines, or Akron, since every community has its foibles and unique characters.

No one argues that because William Faulkner's fictitious Yoknapatawpha County is in Mississippi, it is absent of universal truths or reader appeal. Stories are stories, regardless of setting, and they may be very good stories because of the setting.

At workshops and seminars there have been questions and references to book reviews, and new writers wonder how to get their own works reviewed. I tell them that publishers always send out new releases to a list of reviewing media. The downside is that because of the glut of books craving attention of book editors, few will get noticed. And of those that do get reviewed, there's a chance the published notice will be negative. Authors need to be prepared for the possibility of cranky assessment of the books they've devoted countless hours to craft, only to realize that all that work has failed to impress some critic who tells them in 300 words that they've wasted their time.

Obviously, we authors much prefer positive evaluations, but must contend with negative as well. However, negative reviews have become much rarer these days, because book review sections have been eliminated in many daily papers, so most published reviews tend toward the positive. In years past, many papers utilized freelance reviewers (I've been one myself), but newspaper budget cuts have eliminated many freelance contributors, leaving only the editor and news services to critique new books. With book editors on overload, they may be unwilling to crack the covers of tomes they sense they may not like. I get that: so many books and so little time, is it worthwhile to even look at something one is not likely to enjoy or find stimulating?

Criticisms of my books have run the gamut. The "brilliantly written" book from an Ottawa, Canada, newspaper was "predictable," according to another reviewer, and its thesis brought a "So what?" response. You can't quibble with individual assessments of your work, unless the reviewer makes factual errors. Even then, your letter to the critic or the page editor will likely come off as whiny.

Still, authors should be grateful for any reviews, because most books published today aren't mentioned in any media. Recent reports indicate about 330,000 books are published in the U. S. each year, with only a tiny fraction of those receiving even one published review—excluding consumer reviews placed online.

More bad news: roughly eighty percent of published books lose money (thus far only four of my books earned enough to recover advances), and today's book has less than a one percent chance of being carried in more than a handful of bookstores. The exception is for books that have strong community connections. Authors who live in the area, or whose story is situated there, have a decent chance of at least denting the local market. Moreover, today's authors are expected to take the lion's share of promotion by visiting book stores, meeting with book clubs, developing an author's web page, and making full use of available online venues. Some manage on their own to arrange interviews on local radio or television stations. Reclusive Emily Dickinson, who couldn't bear self-aggrandizement in her lifetime, would hardly matter in today's marketplace either. Some marketing director would be phoning her and saying "Geez, Em, you gotta get out and do some readings, shake some hands, schmooze a little. Try to tell some jokes too. I mean, babe, this is a business and you gotta get it together."

Alas, poor Emily, and alas, any writer who isn't media and Internet savvy today.

CHAPTER 17

A POETIC VENTURE, AND ASSOCIATIVE AGNOSIA

Though I have barely ventured into writing poems, I did put my toe in the water, so to speak, following my second Anderson Center residency in 1999. Being around poets for a whole month on two separate occasions spurred enthusiasm for the form in a way not experienced before. Perhaps my trepidation stemmed from the fact that my younger brother David is a published poet who has done readings with his friend Robert Pinsky, former Poet Laureate of the United States. David is the family poet who dabbles in essays while I reverse that, primarily concentrating on essays and short stories. I never considered myself a poet, and still don't, but following my last Anderson Center sojourn, I returned home and during a slow stretch when other work stalled, I completed three poems in one month, and to my delight, editors accepted each one.

A friend related the story of his sister purchasing a rural property outside of town, who was told there might be an issue of concern. The seller told her there was a Finnish fellow who'd lived there in an out building for nearly a decade. The woman, Angela, in my poem, thought he was joking until she took possession of the home. The Finn indeed squatted in an unheated shed. Angela tried over a period of months, the friend said, to convince the squatter that he should find a place of his own because she fretted about conditions in the shed. But the Finn proved helpful and was good with her horses. Long story short, they were married within six months.

Try as I might over a period of many months, I failed to force Angela and her Finn into a short story. I was unable to generate fiction from what was very loosely based on a real-life observation of a woman who felt "stuck" with a man who resided on the property she had purchased and was reluctant to leave. After numerous false starts, what I assumed would be a story emerged as the poem "Angela's Finn," and was included in the initial annual volume *The Great American Poetry Show*.

The second poem, "At the Hotel Giotto, Assisi," was influenced by a finger dancer on the Piazza Navona in Rome, who asked my wife to shine a flashlight on his hands while they "danced." Except for that snippet, the rest of the poem is imagination—again a failed story about a melancholy man lamenting the fact that he brought his wife to Rome to reinvigorate their relationship, and she left him for the finger dancer.

The final poem, "Joe Montana at the Louvre," came from noticing the Hall of Fame quarterback in the museum with his wife and daughters, and how a group of American high school students left their docent and pursued the football icon down the gallery and stairs before he disappeared into the Mona Lisa room.

That I wrote the poems at all was something of a surprise since I had never attempted to craft verses before. I suppose I should have been heartened and gone on to write others, but upon re-examining those poems, I discovered that what I'd actually created were stories in free verse. I am not apparently inspired by nature or relationships so much as by observations and snippets of conversation, which are grist for more serious poets. The trio of verses worked for me only after I couldn't turn those subjects into stories or essays.

I learned that like an athlete who makes a brilliant play or has a terrific season, the well wasn't deep enough to sustain a career, and brother David remains the family poet.

But another factor recently occurred upon my discovery that I'm on the visual agnosia spectrum. It's nothing serious, but it hinders my ability to vividly describe scenes.

Several years ago I began to comprehend a mild, life-long disorder after watching a televised interview with film and TV writer/producer Aaron Sorkin. During the program, Sorkin said he wrote radio scripts, not screenplays, because he could not visualize the stories he created. "I hand the script off to others who fill in settings and background," he said. Listening to Sorkin's words, I realized I'd endured a similar affliction that I kept secret for fear of embarrassment.

During my 1940s and 50s elementary school years in Duluth, I was the only boy in my class who could not identify automobiles by make. Chevrolets, Fords, Plymouths—all appeared indistinct to me. I couldn't recognize one from another, unless I happened to spot the name on its hood or trunk.

From Kindergarten through sixth grade, I don't think any of my pals knew I could only discern cars by color and size. These were kids whose fathers took them downtown to Bolton-Swanby Chevrolet or Sterling Motors, the Ford dealership, to look at the new models each year, and many of them would report on the visits during show and tell.

Boys back then were universally car-crazy, and auto-centered conversations were always energized, and, in my mind, inevitable whenever three or four mates were together on the playground or street corners. But none of my peers were aware of my inability to identify cars because I always feigned interest when discussions turned automotive, and I sometimes drew attention when mentioning that my uncle Frank annually purchased a new Pontiac. Pontiacs were beyond the financial reach of families in our blue-collar neighborhood, and mates thought Frank must be rich. A bachelor, Frank owned a successful dry-cleaning establishment. He took week-long fishing junkets at Canada resorts, though what most impressed me about my uncle was that as a young visitor to New York he saw Babe Ruth hit two homeruns against the Washington Senators at Yankee Stadium.

During my fifth grade year I was appointed to the prestigious school-crossing patrol at U.S. Grant Elementary School. This was a big deal, as most members of the patrol were sixth graders. A fifth-grade boy would be appointed lieutenant and would ascend to captain the next year, with a special badge indicating this position. I was pleased and proud to have been selected, but became anxious following a meeting of the patrol with a local police officer who trained crossing guards for all city elementary schools. The officer congratulated the "police boys" as we were called then, and said he was sure we'd do well during the school year. He reminded us to be on time for duties, and not to leave our stations until the last youngster had crossed at our intersection. Then he said, "You probably won't have to do this, but every now and then it could be that someone will drive through your stop sign. Should that ever happen, get the make of the car and try to get the license number, then report it to your principal who will call the police department."

I panicked. There was an off-chance I might catch a license number, but I wouldn't know whether the car was a Ford, Chevy, Plymouth, or Buick. Though I could identify station wagons, convertibles, and coupes, I couldn't discern their manufacturer. At best I might say, "The car was gray, and the front bumper was rusty." Luckily, there were no stop sign violations during the two years I served on the school-boy patrol, neither for me, nor any other lads at their posts.

As years passed, however, my car-identification issue diminished. Not that I was brought up to speed, but rather teenage boys no longer stood around challenging each other over who first spotted an approaching 1947 Chevy or 1949 Nash.

In all other boyhood activities and pursuits, I was well within the norm. I was a decent athlete and even co-captained our high school baseball team. I participated in activities and enjoyed a wide circle of friends. And by the time I finished junior high school, the inability to recognize cars wasn't on my radar.

When my unseeing resurfaced, I was in college, but now, it had nothing to do with cars. I discovered I could not "see" art. Paintings were visible, of course, and I could describe any that were realistic—portraits, landscapes, seascapes—but beyond that I was completely at sea. I barely passed a required art appreciation course as a sophomore because I could only superficially assess fine art. I was unable to perceive symbolism in collages, paintings, or sculptures, or comprehend the artists' angst, pain, or joie de vivre, which continues to vex my art-teacher wife. Our European junkets inevitably bring us to iconic museums, galleries, and cathedrals, and I always get "museumed out." After viewing major works by the masters, my unarticulated thoughts are along the lines of, "Oh, another Leonardo, another Rembrandt, more Picasso, another Modigliani." Judy, on the other hand, can be moved to tears by some of Monet's last paintings, and no museum visit is ever long enough for her.

The writers with whom I associate are also art connoisseurs, and I have often felt like an island among those knowledgeable about fine art. I've read books about the subject and acquired a dilettantish confidence to utter a brief comment now and then, but that's it.

Since Aaron Sorkin's revelation regarding his inability to visualize scripts, I started feeling less alone in my not seeing. Over the last forty-odd years, my métiers have been short stories and essays, and almost nothing I've published reveals much description. Dialogue is central to my fiction, while ideas and memories dominate my essays. I was a broadcasting major in grad school decades ago and concentrated on radio. But even by then, the old-time soap operas, mysteries, adventure shows, and comedies had long since moved to television, and the only writing for radio consisted of news and advertising commercials, which held scant appeal for me.

Poring over some of my early and mostly unpublished works, I find essays and stories bereft of description, save the obvious: colors, size, distance and the like. I was unable to capture visual settings in writings. Re-examining those pieces, I flashed back to grade school, standing mute while other boys easily recognized passing cars.

My particular disorder is defined as impairment in recognition of visually presented objects, and is not related to visual acuity. It is called associative agnosia—an inability to distinguish certain objects even with apparent perception and knowledge of them. It is mainly manifested when I look at automobiles and art. But I also cannot interpret blueprints; I'm unable to visualize what the floor plan will look like upon completion. I only see lines on a grid.

My wife oversees any remodeling or landscape projects we undertake.

In a larger sense, what does it mean to learn I have a touch of associative agnosia? Some years ago I was asked to adapt my book, *The Lynchings in Duluth*, for a screenplay. For months I struggled to complete a script, to no avail. My effort wasn't working, and I abandoned the project. I had failed at a task that might have been somewhat challenging but pleasurable to other writers. I found it frustrating. At least now I have the associative agnosia excuse for not attempting screenplays, and also declining to spend much time in art galleries and museums. I hope that when Judy or my art aficionado friends ask me to accompany them to exhibits and shows, they'll understand that my associative agnosia inhibits my appreciation and understanding of visual art.

I'm okay with this, though I'd like to think I'd tackle another screenwriting attempt if, like Aaron Sorkin, I could access gifted supernumeraries to fill in the visual blanks of any screenplay I might conjure.

This knowledge also gave me slight comfort in reflecting back on my screenwriting attempt to adapt *The Lynchings in Duluth*. Like Aaron Sorkin, I couldn't capture the visualization. But all wasn't naught. I was recently commissioned to develop a radio play from the book by the public station at St. Cloud State University. I was able to do this, and the play, *Trial By Mob*, has been broadcast by the St. Cloud station and others in the consortium of non-National Public Radio affiliates.

CHAPTER 18

A WRITER'S ROOMS

ONE OF THE MANY PROVOCATIVE POINTS RAISED BY ANNIE Dillard in her fascinating book, *The Writing Life*, concerns appropriate workspaces for writers. Those that are pleasant and appealing, she argues, are to be avoided. "One wants a room with no view, so imagination can meet memory in the dark."

Hearkening to her advice, as a fledgling writer the first space I used exclusively for writing was a cramped back bedroom, the size of a large closet, in the tiny cabin my wife and I rented on Tainter Lake in Colfax, Wisconsin. The room had no view of the lake; its solitary undersized aperture looked out upon a thatch of gnarled pin oaks and box elders, whose branches and leaves shrouded the window, letting in only dim eastern light. Since I taught in the morning at a nearby college, I wrote most afternoons in that grim cell while voices of men at leisure fishing for crappies from the bank below the cottage drifted through my window.

I didn't produce much memorable prose in that dark back bedroom. During my tenure there I seldom looked at the lake or considered its spectacular circle of red and fire-gold September maple leaves. I was monkish in my devotion to craft, dutifully churning out melancholy essays and angst-driven stories that mostly went unpublished.

My next writing room was in Peru, New York, where I fashioned a desk from a door mounted on cinder blocks. The room was unpainted and a small window faced Moore Drive and the home across the street that looked exactly like ours—like all the homes in the development.

In far upstate New York, where I kept regular hours as a media specialist at the college in Plattsburgh, I rose at five each weekday in order to manage a couple hours of writing before heading off to work.

However, I managed little of note there, except two travel essays and several other short pieces that were published before we moved to Minnesota, where I assumed a basement office, sans windows, with a single heating vent. I kept my door-on-cinder-blocks desk. The temperature never seemed to rise above sixty degrees summer or winter. During the winters I covered my feet in an old blanket while I wrote. Summers saw me descend the stairs wearing a sweatshirt on all but the warmest of days. Looking back on what I composed in those dwellings, I'm struck by the bleak visions of my stories and essays.

This brings me to the present: a spacious front room office, facing my neighborhood of children at play, and middle-aged couples with dogs on leashes or young families—offspring unleashed—walking the street. A woman regularly jogs by with her Doberman, a well-mannered beast, who doubtless would become less so should anyone approach his mistress with malevolent intent. A semi-retired gentleman ambles from house to house engaging in gossip with stay-at-home soccer moms. My office here is well-lighted, and I view the street through three large four-foot windows. Two peregrine falcons have survived dives into them. I've also observed bald eagles overhead, and the occasional great horned owl perches in the ring of red oaks in our yard. Now and then foxes and the occasional coyote trot through my wife's delphiniums.

With all due respect to Annie Dillard, my imagination requires the meeting of memory in light, in brilliance, in motion, in sound, all of which come to me in this present place. My work has evolved from its former gloom and cynicism to being occasionally downright silly. Since I've been able to look outside whenever I lift my head from the computer screen, my work has moved more smoothly, has become more fun.

Since arriving here more than twenty-five years ago, I've published two books of mirth and seven other volumes, in addition to several dozen stories and essays. Neither my fictional characters nor I are much possessed of angst worth expressing, though one reviewer said my novel was angst-driven.

I suppose while one can remove the writer from his angst, it may be harder to remove angst from the writer. After all, the writer is beset with doubt about the quality of his work, stews about its acceptance by an editor, frets further about reactions from readers, and worries whether the advance will cover expenses and other costs piled on credit cards over the past six months.

For me, Ms. Dillard's dictum about the writer's space doesn't apply. I'm already rather dour by nature, given to gray moods, which are fed by gray days and gray spaces. The writing I produced during my days in spare and melancholy environs reflected my mood, and fueled my tendency to be cranky and unapproachable. Give me instead a well-lighted space with pictures and posters on the wall, surrounded by books, classical or jazz CDs, a mug of Darjeeling at the ready, and the world as it appears on Lily Street—walkers, joggers, falcons, and foxes—and I'm usually eager to begin my work day, prepared, in the words of J. M. Barrie, to "Greet the future with a cheer."

CHAPTER 19

WHY WRITE?

ANOTHER QUESTION I'M OFTEN ASKED WHEN I TALK AT MIDDLE and high school classrooms is, why did you decide to be a writer? The simple answer is, I write because I can't not write, and feel compelled to do so in the same manner of serious musicians or fine artists, dancers, and actors. Most practitioners of these arts cannot earn a middle-class living doing what they love. Nonetheless, many are driven to try, and try, and try, and will stay the course for years without managing anything close to a significant breakthrough. And even those whose names are familiar to many people have experienced minimal financial rewards. I'm sometimes a bit surprised to learn that a performer I've long respected has been made almost destitute because of a serious health issue. Benefits are often staged to help these artists pay medical expenses.

Those of us who aren't earning a living wage from writing or acting or painting or music or dancing may envy those who do, but we have traded that for the security of a regular paycheck, health insurance, a retirement or 401K plan, and can afford amenities like a new car every five or ten years, and can purchase a home. Many arts practitioners cannot. Yet they soldier on.

I recently calculated without knowing the specifics of her contracts that J. K. Rowling, if receiving a conservative estimate five dollars per book sold, earns more royalties in a single day of sales for new Harry Potter books—more than $220,000—than I have in fifty years of selling what I write. And of course, she may be receiving even more than that.

Are we after fame and wealth? Most likely so, but I long ago learned to accept reality. I would be neither famous nor wealthy. I'm reminded of the time several years ago when I was the designated writer at a suburban middle school Career Day. In my first session, a sixth-grade boy asked me if I was a famous author. In return I asked if he had ever heard of me. When he said "No," I replied he'd answered his own question.

I had a similar experience at a recent social gathering during which the hostess introduced me to other guests as a "famous author." Some of them may have felt uneasy because, like the middle-school kid, my name was equally unfamiliar to them.

For the record, just one of my nine previously published books has sold upward of 30,000 copies, and that total combines the sales of hardcover and paperback editions. Thirty thousand books won't place a work on best-seller lists or get its author on "60 Minutes" or the "Today Show."

The sixth grader, the hostess, and quite a few other folks somehow assume that all published authors are equally celebrated. And I suspect that a few students who enrolled in my writing classes also presumed that fame accompanies publication.

T'ain't necessarily so. I can walk into the community library several blocks from my home and go unrecognized by the staff. My name isn't familiar to them either, despite the presence of seven of my books on their shelves.

Ditto at local chain bookstores and a handful of independents. As an author of midlist titles, I suspect I'm in the same boat as most other writers who have been fortunate enough to publish a book or two.

While publication may not equate with fame, it also may not even win esteem from the author's own family. My daughters never seemed much impressed with the fact that I'm an author. I think they regarded me solely as the happy-go-melancholy guy who happened to be their father.

But at least my girls know I'm a writer. I heard once about another writer seated at the table at a large family reunion picnic. The conversation centered on a provocative story in the current issue of a major national magazine. The writer was asked if he had seen the piece. "I not only saw it," he said, "I wrote it."

Fame is not what most writers anticipate. Fame is for rockers, film actors, network news anchors. Star status is occasionally accorded writers like Stephen King or Alice Walker, but every now and then, even midlist authors flirt with fame and can be seduced.

The perks and bonuses, as well as name and face recognition, do occur for some writers. But they're hardly the reasons we are compelled to write. Most of us aren't arbiters of public tastes, and even if we were, we still might not be able to tailor our work to satisfy those palates.

It's probably for the best. The really important literature was never written with expectations of fame and fortune for the author. Most of us toil in relative anonymity. Our reward is in completing our work. Our bonus might be publication. Fame? I've received a lot of acclaim around the neighborhood lately. But it has nothing to do with writing. I caught a ten-pound lake trout last fall, and half the folks on the block have cornered me, insisting I tell them in great detail how I accomplished so wondrous a feat.

Actually, a ten-pound lake trout isn't that impressive. A trophy catch would have to hit about twenty pounds. So far, though the ten-pounder is the best I've done, despite investing countless hours over the last half-century trying to land at least one brag-able leviathan.

I console myself by reflecting that my trout was a decent catch, and there are thousands of anglers who haven't equaled that. Similarly, there must be scores of frustrated writers and authors who might hearken to William Faulkner as they desperately seek to publish just once in their lives. Compared with them, I'm lucky indeed and at this stage in life, happily settle for it.

In summing up, what does the literary life look like for this midlist author? The prolific novelist Georges Simenon once observed, "Writing is not a profession, but a vocation of unhappiness." In an essay in his book, *Crooning*, the late John Gregory Dunne defined writing as "manual labor of the mind; a job like laying pipe."

The literary life I fancied was depicted in the *Paris Review Writers at Work* interviews. It consisted of midmorning hours at the typewriter with breaks for tea or coffee, lunch, then afternoons reserved for correspondence, reading, light research, perhaps a tennis match and twilight cocktails prior to the evening's soiree, which would be a gathering of stimulating glitterati.

What I didn't understand in my callow youth was that few authors earn enough in royalties to support that literary lifestyle.

After five decades of scrounging around the edges of literary life, managing to publish the occasional book, story, or essay while holding jobs with regular paychecks and benefits, I've yet to enjoy the unhurried and intellectually engaging existence of those *Paris Review* authors. I've made few acquaintances among other writers—a fact I rued until I came across another of John Gregory Dunne's observations: "Writers do not make easy friends of one another; they are professional carpers, too competitive, mean-spirited and envious for the demands of lasting friendship."

In any case, I've lived in working-class communities, where literature was not intrinsically valued and fellow writers were scarce or nonexistent. My companions tended to be geezers with a passion for fishing bass and trout.

I did attend one literary soiree. During my tenure as a stringer for *The New York Times*, I was invited to a book publication party at a boisterous bar in Minneapolis, where the recently published author regularly took a liquid lunch. Someone had set up a table containing three blocks of cheese, a cleaver to chunk it with, and two platters of broken crackers. To wash down the viands, we could choose a tumbler of jug wine or a Styrofoam cup of thin coffee. The author's pals gravitated toward the jugs. A stack of his books on the floor near the table went largely unnoticed.

I still believe there must be soirees and literary lunches such as existed in my imagination—Algonquin-type round tables where writers exchange bon mots and swap anecdotes about editors, books, and their own work; where they sip Napoleon brandy and nibble bruschetta with sun-dried tomatoes and chevre.

Perhaps one can't taste the literary life though, unless one is fully devoted to the profession, and for most of the last fifty-plus years I've written part-time.

Twenty years ago when I was offered an early retirement incentive, I quit teaching and have devoted myself to the quest of living the literary life. I've redoubled my efforts to publish stories and essays in major slicks and prestigious quarterlies.

My friends are still geezer fishermen.

I go to bed later now than I did when I held a regular job; I may sleep in and rarely rush my morning ablutions. I read the papers, take second and third cups of Darjeeling or coffee, and sit at the keyboard by nine. I listen to jazz or classical CDs while I write.

Then I work till noon and reheat yesterday's pasta or chowder for lunch. Except for the occasional political solicitation or one of my geezer buddies urging me to get off my duff and get serious about fishing now that I'm retired, the phone rarely rings. Literary conversation has been sporadic at best. The closest I came to one was a while back when a gentleman representing one of the boards where I attend church phoned. He understood I enjoyed writing and was pleased because he said that hardly anybody wanted to write these days. He wondered if I'd be willing to assume the role of congregation secretary.

I declined, saying my handwriting was illegible and even I couldn't transcribe it if I waited more than an hour after taking notes.

He sighed. "Yeah, me too. Now my wife's niece does calligraphy. Just beautiful. Makes her own Christmas cards."

It never occurred to this fellow that one of his acquaintances might actually write creatively. Writing to him meant mere scribing, and he'd heard I was good at it.

Still, retirement has enabled me to focus my days at the keyboard. I break for tea or coffee. I read. I work out at the local YMCA. I sulk.

Some years ago I received month-long residencies at the Anderson Center for Interdisciplinary Studies in Red Wing, Minnesota, and lived in the large old house built by the man who invented the process for manufacturing puffed wheat and puffed rice. During the first of those I eagerly anticipated provocative discussions with other writers and artists, as well as the opportunity to critique each other's work during evening salons. I was not disappointed, and I cherish the time I spent there surrounded by people keenly interested in how my writing was progressing. But after returning home I thought that living at the Anderson Center was probably as close as I'll ever come to the literary life I constructed from those *Paris Review* interviews.

I possess an ample paperback library that must be worth hundreds of dollars, despite the ripped covers and dog-eared pages. Since my retirement I've augmented it with remaindered hardcover volumes, and the home office where I work looks like a writer's room, brimming with what my wife calls creative clutter.

Otherwise, there's been little change in this writer's life. I deal with editorial rejections, occasional acceptances, and a paucity of literary discussion. No soirees, few lunches with agents and editors. Perhaps the literary life is not about hobnobbing with editors and discussing film options with Hollywood producers. Most likely it is simply my job—the task of all writers—an ongoing effort to lay more pipe.

ADDENDUM

As a writer and former teacher of writing, I've often been asked what a writer's most important virtue would be. The answer is simple: discipline. Many talented writers have never published, but writers not blessed with brilliance publish because they are determined to write something every day or every week.

Consider this: In order to write for publication, you must become a writer. At first glance this seems obvious. But most aspiring writers do not consider themselves to be writers. They regard themselves as persons who may one day become writers. They think they aren't real writers until they start publishing.

In my teaching days I always told students that no matter what their stations in life, they must consider themselves writers. Most of us who manage to regularly publish our work do not earn our primary incomes from writing. Among our numbers are teachers, nurses, engineers, salespersons, cooks—the gamut of workaday positions. And our identifications are usually derived from our main occupations. But I urged my students to change their principal status to writer, if they're serious about writing.

I sometimes asked students to identify in a priority ranking, one through ten, the roles they assume in their daily lives. Since most of them were women, they mentioned their major responsibilities as wife or mother, then daughter, friend, and somewhere in the middle or near the end they listed their occupations. Most of those women placed careers below relationships. There's nothing wrong with this, but it may impede one's capacity to write. If writing ranks seventh, it likely receives minimal attention and effort.

Prior to my retirement as a college instructor, I was not a teacher who wrote, but a writer who happened to teach. That distinction gave perspective to my life, and enabled me to become disciplined as a writer. If I'd been a teacher who wrote occasionally, others, including my family, would have few qualms about infringing upon my writing time. My writing would have been a hobby, like sketching or gardening or golf.

Most of us who engage in hobbies aren't compulsive about them. We see them as spare-time activities. But writing—at least writing for publication—requires serious effort. We don't write in our spare time; we set aside time for writing. And in this regard, we must be selfish. Writing time may not be interrupted with impunity. It belongs to the writer. What that means for many of us is that we make sacrifices to do our writing. We may have to reduce or eliminate activities that keep us from writing.

Our partners must come to understand and appreciate this. That which is best about me results from my being a writer. It is, I think, much of what my wife found appealing about me. Writing defines me: It is who I am. To give this up, and the time it consumes, is to stop being my best self.

Years ago, when I was a new writer, I would rise at five and write for ninety minutes before heading to my regular job. I wasn't happy rising before dawn, but this was the only way I was going to meet my writing goal, which was to complete two to two and a half pages each morning. This practice curtailed my social life, since I had to be in bed by ten most evenings.

The sacrifices made in order to write, however, do not guarantee success. We can't even be sure they will lead to publication. I've heard editors say that they've received submissions from certain writers for years, and those submissions are nowhere near publishable quality. Yet who can tell if the next story, the next book, won't be right on target?

You and I are the only ones who know when to throw in the towel—be it after five years or forty of fruitless attempts to publish.

Finally, forget inspiration. It's fickle and unpredictable, and you'll get precious little writing done if you sit around and wait for it. We can do little to influence inspiration, but we can discipline ourselves to establish writing as a priority in our lives.

I encountered writing students whose talents exceeded my own, but to my knowledge, haven't published. The only difference between me and those students is that I write regularly and they don't. The person who finds his or her way to publication is the person who has formed the writing habit and who insists on writing's priority in his or her life.

* * *

Having said this, I conclude with a quote from Henry Wood, he of *A Sawdust Heart*. When I asked the old fellow what one final thought he had about his hardscrabble decades in show business, he said (and I second it regarding the writer's trade), "It's been grand, and I have no regrets."

Finis

ACKNOWLEDGMENTS

S OME MATERIAL IN THIS TEXT PREVIOUSLY APPEARED IN OTHER venues, but was substantially re-constructed for this book. These include: *A View from the Loft, Minnesota Literature, Los Angeles Times Book Review, The World & I, The Writer, America, The Minneapolis Star Tribune,* also in the book *Zenith City: Stories from Duluth* (University of Minnesota Press, 2014) and in workshops and speeches presented over the past twenty years.

I also thank Bob Lacy, who critiqued this manuscript and offered many useful suggestions. I shall always be grateful to the late Mike Derr for his constant encouragement throughout the 1990s and early 2000s during his tenure as editor of *America West Airlines Magazine*.

ABOUT THE AUTHOR

A DULUTH, MINNESOTA NATIVE, MICHAEL FEDO IS A GRADUATE of the University of Minnesota-Duluth, and taught 10th and 11th grade English at Duluth Denfeld High School, coaching tennis and football for two years before attending graduate school at Kent State University in Ohio, where he received an M. A. in broadcasting and theater. He spent the next 32 years teaching at colleges in Ohio, New York, Wisconsin, and Minnesota. During his more than five-decade writing career, he has published hundreds of articles and essays in *The New York Times, Christian Science Monitor, Los Angeles Times, Reader's Digest, McCall's, Runner's World, America,* and elsewhere. His short stories have appeared in *Gray's Sporting Journal, American Way, America West Airlines Magazine, North American Review, December,* and in many other literary quarterlies. He is a former book reviewer for the *Minneapolis Star Tribune,* and for ten years taught writing at The Loft Literary Center in Minneapolis. His essays have been broadcast on Minnesota, Wisconsin, and Florida Public Radio. *Don't Quit Your Day Job: The Adventures of a Midlist Author* is his tenth book.